MATH
INSTANT ASSESSMENTS
for Data Tracking
Grade 5

Credits
Author: Redeana Davis Smith

Visit *carsondellosa.com* for correlations to Common Core, state, national, and Canadian provincial standards.

Carson-Dellosa Publishing, LLC
PO Box 35665
Greensboro, NC 27425 USA
carsondellosa.com

978-1-4838-3614-0
01-339161151

Table of Contents

✦ Assessment and Data Tracking ✦

Data tracking is an essential element in modern classrooms. Teachers are often required to capture student learning through both formative and summative assessments. They then must use the results to guide teaching, remediation, and lesson planning and provide feedback to students, parents, and administrators. Because time is always at a premium in the classroom, it is vital that teachers have the assessments they need at their fingertips. The assessments need to be suited to the skill being assessed as well as adapted to the stage in the learning process. This is true for an informal checkup at the end of a lesson or a formal assessment at the end of a unit.

This book will provide the tools and assessments needed to determine your students' level of mastery throughout the school year. The assessments are both formal and informal and include a variety of formats—pretests and posttests, flash cards, prompt cards, traditional tests, and exit tickets. Often, there are several assessment options for a single skill or concept to allow you the greatest flexibility when assessing understanding. Simply select the assessment that best fits your needs, or use them all to create a comprehensive set of assessments for before, during, and after learning.

Incorporate Instant Assessments into your daily plans to streamline the data-tracking process and keep the focus on student mastery and growth.

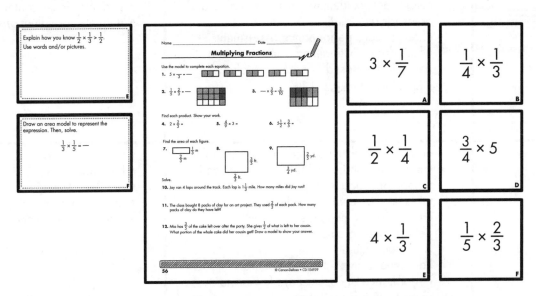

A variety of instant assessments for multiplying fractions

Types of Assessment

Assessment usually has a negative association because it brings to mind tedious pencil-and-paper tests and grading. However, it can take on many different forms and be a positive, integral part of the year. Not all assessments need to be formal, nor do they all need to be graded. Choose the type of assessment to use based on the information you need to gather. Then, you can decide if or how it should be graded.

	What Does It Look Like?	Examples
Formative Assessment	• occurs during learning • is administered frequently • is usually informal and not graded • identifies areas of improvement • provides immediate feedback so a student can make adjustments promptly, if needed • allows teachers to rethink strategies, lesson content, etc., based on current student performance • is process-focused • has the most impact on a student's performance	• in-class observations • exit tickets • reflections and journaling • homework • student-teacher conferences • student self-evaluations
Interim Assessment	• occurs occasionally • is more formal and usually graded • feedback is not immediate, though still fairly quick • helps teachers identify gaps in teaching and areas for remediation • often includes performance assessments, which are individualized, authentic, and performance-based in order to evaluate higher-level thinking skills	• in-class observations • exit tickets • reflections and journaling • homework • student-teacher conferences • student self-evaluations
Summative Assessment	• occurs once learning is considered complete • the information is used by the teacher and school for broader purposes • takes time to return a grade or score • can be used to compare a student's performance to others • is product-focused • has the least impact on a student's performance since there are few or no opportunities for retesting	• cumulative projects • final portfolios • quarterly testing • end-of-the-year testing • standardized testing

How to Use This Book

The assessments in this book follow a few different formats, depending on the skill or concept being assessed. Use the descriptions below to familiarize yourself with each unique format and get the most out of Instant Assessments all year long.

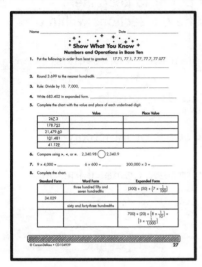

Show What You Know

Each domain begins with a pair of *Show What You Know* tests. Both tests follow the same format and include the same types of questions so they can be directly compared to show growth. Use them as a pretest and posttest. Or, use one as a test at the end of a unit and use the second version as a retest for students after remediation.

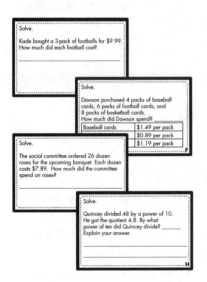

Exit Tickets

Each domain ends with exit tickets that cover the variety of concepts within the domain. Exit tickets are very targeted questions designed to assess understanding of specific skills, so they are ideal formative assessments to use at the end of a lesson. Exit tickets do not have space for student names, allowing teachers to gather information on the entire class without placing pressure on individual students. If desired, have students write their names or initials on the backs of the tickets. Other uses for exit tickets include the following:

- Use the back of each ticket for longer answers, fuller explanations, or extension questions. If needed, students can staple them to larger sheets of paper.
- They can also be used for warm-ups or to find out what students know before a lesson.
- Use the generic exit tickets on pages 7 and 8 for any concept you want to assess. Be sure to fill in any blanks before copying.
- Laminate them and place them in a math center as task cards.
- Use them to play Scoot or a similar review game at the end of a unit.
- Choose several to create a targeted assessment for a skill or set of skills.

Cards

Use the cards as prompts for one-on-one conferencing. Simply copy the cards, cut them apart, and follow the directions preceding each set of cards. Use the lettering to keep track of which cards a student has interacted with.

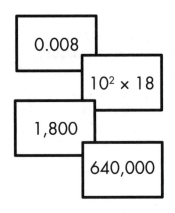

- Copy on card stock and/or laminate for durability.
- Punch holes in the top left corners and place the cards on a book ring to make them easily accessible.
- Copy the sets on different colors of paper to keep them easily separated or to distinguish different sections within a set of cards.
- Easily differentiate by using different amounts or levels of cards to assess a student.
- Write the answers on the backs of cards to create self-checking flash cards.
- Place them in a math center as task cards or matching activities.
- Use them to play Scoot or a similar review game at the end of a unit.

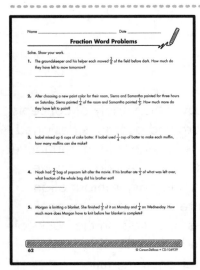

Assessment Pages

The reproducible assessment pages are intended for use as a standard test of a skill. Use them in conjunction with other types of assessment to get a full picture of a student's level of understanding. They can also be used for review or homework.

Math Talk Prompt Cards

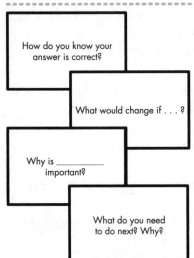

Use the math talk prompt cards on pages 9 and 10 to prompt math discussions that can be used to informally assess students' levels of understanding. Use the math talk prompts to encourage reflection and deeper understanding of math concepts throughout the year.

- Copy on card stock and/or laminate for durability.
- Punch holes in the top left corners and place the cards on a book ring to keep them easily accessible.
- Use them for journaling prompts.
- Place them in a math center to be used with other activities.

Exit Tickets

Exit tickets are a useful formative assessment tool that you can easily work into your day. You can choose to use a single exit ticket at the end of the day or at the end of each lesson. Simply choose a ticket below and make one copy for each student. Then, have students complete the prompt and present them to you as their ticket out of the door. Use the student responses to gauge overall learning, create small remediation groups, or target areas for reteaching. A blank exit ticket is included on page 8 so you can create your own exit tickets as well.

What stuck with you today?

_____

_____

_____

_____

_____

List three facts you learned today. Put them in order from most important to least important.

1. _____

   _____

2. _____

   _____

3. _____

   _____

The first thing I'll tell my family about today is

_____

_____

_____

_____

_____ .

The most important thing I learned today is

_____

_____

_____

_____

_____ .

Color the face that shows how you feel about understanding today's lesson.

Explain why. _____

_____

Summarize today's lesson in 10 words or less.

_____

_____

_____

_____

One example of _____ is _____

_____

_____

_____

_____ .

One question I still have is _____

_____

_____

_____

_____ .

How will understanding _____

_____

help you in real life? _____

_____

_____

_____ .

One new word I learned today is _____

_____ .

It means _____

_____

_____

_____ .

Draw a picture related to the lesson.
Add a caption.

_____

_____

If today's lesson were a song, the title would

be _____

_____

because _____

_____ .

The answer is _____ .

What is the question? _____

_____

_____

_____

_____

Math Talk Prompts

Use these prompts when observing individual students in order to better understand their thinking and depth of understanding of a concept. These cards may also be used during whole-class lessons or in small remediation groups to encourage students to explain their thinking with different concepts.

How did you solve it?	What strategy did you use?
How could you solve it a different way?	Can you repeat that in your own words?
Explain your thinking.	Did you use any key words? Which ones?

Can you explain why you chose to do that?

Why did you choose to add/subtract/ multiply/divide?

How do you know your answer is correct?

How can you prove your answer?

Is this like any other problems you have solved? How?

What would change if . . . ?

Why is _____ important?

What do you need to do next? Why?

✦ Show What You Know ✦
Operations and Algebraic Thinking

1. Which expression correctly shows *eleven times the sum of four and three*?

    ◯ $11 \times 4 + 3$ ◯ $11 \times (4 + 3)$

    ◯ $4 + 3 \times 11$ ◯ $4 + (3 \times 11)$

2. Solve.

$$(6 + 10) \div (4 \times 2)$$

3. If $a = 9 \times (4 + 2)$ and $b = 9 \times (6 + 2)$, which of the following is true?

    ◯ $a < b$

    ◯ $a > b$

    ◯ $a = b$

4. Complete each pattern. Then, record the rule for each pattern.

0, 3, 6, 9, _____, _____, _____

Rule _____

3.1, 4.1, 5.1, _____, _____, _____

Rule _____

1, 10, 100, _____, _____, _____

Rule _____

5. Place parentheses in the equation to make it true. Show your work to support your answer.

$$50 \div 2 + 8 - 3 = 2$$

6. What is the value of the expression?

$$(42 + 6) \div 8 \times 5 = _____$$

Use what you know the about the order of operations to explain why your answer is correct.

_____

_____

_____

_____

_____

_____

7. Write an equation for the statement.

Abby is four inches shorter than her sister.

_____

_____

8. Which operation should you perform first to solve $50 \div [28 - (9 \times 2)]$?

○ addition

○ multiplication

○ division

○ subtraction

9. Which expression does not have a value of 6?

○ $3 + (7 \times 2) - 11$

○ $(8 \div 4) + (2 + 2)$

○ $4 + 8 \div 2 - 1$

○ $3 \times (6 - 2) \div 2$

10. Complete the chart.

Rule: Add 2	Rule: Add 4	Ordered Pair
0	0	(0, 0)
2	4	(2, 4)

11. Write an expression for *y reduced by 45*.

_____

_____

12. Courtney said that $15 - 2 + 6$ equals 19. Luke said the answer is 13. How did they come up with different answers? Show your work and explain your reasoning.

_____

_____

_____

_____

_____

✦ Show What You Know ✦
Operations and Algebraic Thinking

1. Which expression correctly shows *the difference between the product of six and seven and the sum of four and eight*?

○ $(6 + 7) - (4 \times 8)$ ○ $(6 \times 7) - (4 + 8)$

○ $6 \times (7 + 4) + 8$ ○ $(6 - 7) \times 4 + 8$

2. Solve.

$$(60 - 10) - (5 \times 5)$$

3. If $a = 7 \times (8 + 4)$ and $b = 7 \times (9 + 2)$, which of the following is true?

○ $a < b$

○ $a > b$

○ $a = b$

4. Complete each pattern. Then, record the rule for each pattern.

4, 8, 12, 16, _____, _____, _____

Rule _____

0, 15, 30, _____, _____, _____

Rule _____

$\frac{1}{8}, \frac{3}{8}, \frac{5}{8}$, ___ , ___ , ___

Rule _____

5. Place parentheses in the equation to make it true. Show your work to support your answer.

$$15 - 3 + 40 \div 2 - 8 = 24$$

6. What is the value of the expression?

$$(80 - 17) \div 7 \times 4 = \text{_____}$$

Use what you know the about the order of operations to explain why your answer is correct.

_____

_____

_____

_____

_____

_____

7. Write an equation for the statement.

Quan has twice as many baseball cards as Shane.

_____

_____

8. Which operation should you perform first to solve $3 \times [(3 + 9) - 2]$?

○ addition

○ multiplication

○ division

○ subtraction

9. Which expression does not have a value of 10?

○ $[(30 \div 2) + 2] - 7$

○ $1 + 6 \times 3 \div 2$

○ $100 \div [(18 \div 3) + 4]$

○ $11 - (15 - 10) + 8$

10. Complete the chart.

Rule: Subtract 1	Rule: Add 2	Ordered Pair
8	1	(8, 1)
7	3	(7, 3)

11. Write an expression for *e fewer than 234*.

_____

_____

12. Ms. Diaz said that $12 + 6 \div 3$ equals 14, but Jenny says the answer is 6. Who is correct? Show your work and explain your reasoning.

_____

_____

_____

_____

Numerical Expressions

Use these cards to assess a student's proficiency in evaluating numerical expressions. Cards can be used with the whole class, with small groups, or individually. Present a card and have the student evaluate the expression. Or, choose two cards and have the student tell you which is the greater expression.

$(8 - 6) + 10$ **A**	$(9 + 5) - 3$ **B**
$(5 \times 9) \div (10 + 5)$ **C**	$(3 + 6 \times 6) \div (2 + 1)$ **D**
$(9 + 2) \times (7 + 3)$ **E**	$(24 \div 3) - 5$ **F**
$(2 + 4 + 9) - 8$ **G**	$9 + 2 + 6 \div 3$ **H**

$(8 \times 8) - (11 \times 4)$ <div align="right">I</div>	$3 \times (14 - 8)$ <div align="right">J</div>
$34 - 8 \times 4$ <div align="right">K</div>	$3 + 6 \div 2 - 3$ <div align="right">L</div>
$4 \times 6 + 3 - 9$ <div align="right">M</div>	$10 \div 2 + 4 \times 8$ <div align="right">N</div>
$2 + 5 \times 9 + 5$ <div align="right">O</div>	$20 \div 5 + 3 \times 2$ <div align="right">P</div>
$(4 + 4) \div 2 + 3$ <div align="right">Q</div>	$10 - (3 \times 3) + 7$ <div align="right">R</div>

$8 + 4 \div 2 - 1$ <div align="right">**S**</div>	$2 \times 7 \div (3 + 4)$ <div align="right">**T**</div>
$(14 - 10) \times (20 - 10)$ <div align="right">**U**</div>	$8 + (2 \times 8)$ <div align="right">**V**</div>
$9 - 2 \times 3 + 3$ <div align="right">**W**</div>	$3(4 \times 2)$ <div align="right">**X**</div>
$7 \times 2 + (3 + 5)$ <div align="right">**Y**</div>	$18 \div 2 - 2 \times 3$ <div align="right">**Z**</div>
$5 \times (4 \div 2) + 6$ <div align="right">**AA**</div>	$8 - 4 \times 2 + 2$ <div align="right">**AB**</div>

$(2 \times 2) + (4 \div 2)$

AC

$(12 + 4 \times 3) \div 12$

AD

$(4 + 6) - (2 \times 5)$

AE

$[3 \times (2 + 4)] \div 3$

AF

$8 + (3 \times 4) - 5$

AG

$16 \div 2 + (3 \times 3)$

AH

$7 \times 2 - (5 - 2)$

AI

$9 + [(8 + 2) - 5]$

AJ

$(20 \div 10) \times (14 - 4)$

AK

$[(3 + 4) - 1] \times 4 + 3$

AL

Name _____   Date _____

Expression Matching

Match each mathematical expression to its equivalent number sentence.

_____ **1.** the difference between eight and four multiplied by three

_____ **2.** the sum of nine and eight

_____ **3.** nine increased by a number

_____ **4.** seven less than a number *n*

_____ **5.** the product of 9 and a number *n*

_____ **6.** thirty-two divided by a number *y*

_____ **7.** five more than twice a number

_____ **8.** the product of a number and 6

_____ **9.** seven less than the product of four and five

_____ **10.** fifteen more than *b*

A. $n - 7$

B. $32 \div y$

C. $2n + 5$

D. $b + 15$

E. $9 + 8$

F. $9 + n$

G. $9n$

H. $(8 - 4) \times 3$

I. $(4 \times 5) - 7$

J. $n \times 6$

Numerical Expressions

Place parentheses in each equation to make it true. Show your work.

1. $48 \div 12 \div 4 = 16$	**2.** $20 - 6 \div 2 = 7$
3. $4 \times 7 + 2 = 36$	**4.** $21 + 21 \div 7 = 6$
5. $56 - 15 + 9 = 32$	**6.** $35 - 17 - 11 = 29$
7. $45 - 22 + 9 = 14$	**8.** $60 \div 10 \times 3 = 2$

Name _____ Date _____

Mathematical Expressions

Complete the chart.

1.	360 divided by s	
2.	64 shared among n	
3.	two times the difference of seven and three	
4.		$15 \div (2 + 3)$
5.	156 decreased by b, then multiplied by 3	
6.		$(45 - 15) \div 3$
7.		$10 \times (10 - 6)$
8.	the difference of 12 and 8 divided by 2	
9.		$2 \times (17 + 2)$
10.	twenty-two less than the product of seven and six	

Patterns and Graphing

Complete each table. Then, graph the ordered pairs on the coordinate plane.

1.

Rule: Add 3	Rule: Add 4	Ordered Pair
0	0	(0, 0)

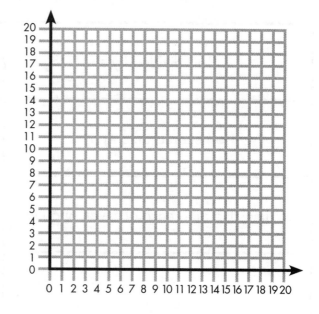

2.

Rule: Add 3	Rule: Add 2	Ordered Pair
0	0	(0, 0)

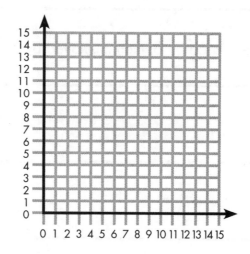

3.

Rule: Add 1	Rule: Add 3	Ordered Pair
0	0	(0, 0)

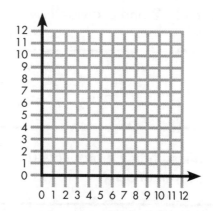

A. Write an equation for the statement.

Antonio is four inches shorter than his older brother.

_____

B. Write a story problem for the expression $4 \times (3 + 7) + 2$.

_____

_____

_____

_____

C. Write a story problem for the expression $(48 \div 4) + 8$.

_____

_____

_____

D. If $b = 3$, solve the expression.

$$[(33 \div b) + 2] - (3 \times 3)$$

E. Without solving, circle the expression that has a greater value. Explain your reasoning.

$$(45,300 + 892) \times 4$$

$$(45,300 + 892) \times 6$$

_____

_____

F. Write the expression for each statement.

fourteen more than the product of two and

seven _____

seven less than the product of seven and four

_____

G. Write the expression in words. Then, solve.

$$40 \div (2 + 8)$$

_____

_____

H. Write the expression in words. Then, solve.

$$3(9 - 2)$$

_____

_____

Colby and Jasper both collect basketball cards. Jasper has three times as many cards as Colby.

Write an algebraic equation to represent the number of cards Jasper has.

_____

I

Nadia can hike 3 miles in one hour.

Write an algebraic expression to show how many miles she can hike in x hours.

_____

J

Solve. Show your work.

$$(36 + 4) \div 8 \times 5$$

K

Solve. Show your work.

$$2 \times (3 + 1) + 2 - 2$$

L

Solve. Show your work.

$$(90 - 48) \div 6 + 2$$

M

Find the patterns to complete the ordered pairs.

(1, 5)   (0, 3)
(3, 15)   (4, 12)
(5, 25)   (8, 48)

(_____ , _____)   (_____ , _____)

(_____ , _____)   (_____ , _____)

N

1, 4, 16, 64, 256, . . .

Rule: _____

How do you know?

_____

_____

O

$$\frac{1}{8}, \frac{3}{8}, \frac{5}{8}, \frac{7}{8}, \frac{9}{8}, \ldots$$

Rule: _____

How do you know?

_____

_____

P

✦ Show What You Know ✦
Number and Operations in Base Ten

1. Write the decimals in order from least to greatest.   33.3, 33.03, 30.33, 33.003, 33.333

_____, _____, _____, _____, _____

2. Round 569.381 to the nearest tenth. _____

3. Rule: Multiply by 10. 0.46, _____, _____, _____, _____

4. Write 5,206.713 in expanded form.

_____

5. Complete the chart with the value and place of each underlined digit.

	Value	Place Value
5<u>6</u>.92		
147.29<u>8</u>		
1,375.<u>6</u>		
101.4<u>8</u>1		
4,<u>2</u>73.449		

6. Compare using **>**, **<**, or **=**.   67.876 ◯ 67.9

7.   7 × 6,000 = _____   8 × 300 = _____   40,000 × 6 = _____

8. Complete the chart.

Standard Form	Word Form	Expanded Form
	fifty-six and two tenths	$(50) + (6) + \left(2 \times \frac{1}{10}\right)$
671.03		
	eleven and eight thousandths	
		$(400) + (7) + \left(5 \times \frac{1}{100}\right) + \left(8 \times \frac{1}{1,000}\right)$

9. 492
  × 6

10. 3,763
  × 5

11. 58
  × 17

12. 394
  × 36

13. 8)456

14. 7)5,782

15. 14)301

16. 15)6,288

17. 22.7
  + 48.87

18. 320
  − 17.6

19. 179.05
  − 80.08

20. 830.07
  + 12.206

21. 6)$8.88

22. 7.8
  × 9

23. 0.6
  × 0.4

24. 5)431

✦ Show What You Know ✦
Number and Operations in Base Ten

1. Write the following in order from least to greatest.   17.71, 77.1, 7.77, 77.7, 77.077

_____, _____, _____, _____, _____

2. Round 3.699 to the nearest hundredth. _____

3. Rule: Divide by 10. 7,000, _____, _____, _____, _____

4. Write 683.402 in expanded form. _____

5. Complete the chart with the value and place of each underlined digit.

	Value	Place Value
26<u>7</u>.3		
178.7<u>5</u>2		
21,479.<u>6</u>0		
1<u>0</u>1.481		
41.12<u>9</u>		

6. Compare using **>**, **<**, or **=**.   2,340.98 ◯ 2,340.9

7. 9 × 4,000 = _____   6 × 600 = _____   300,000 × 3 = _____

8. Complete the chart.

Standard Form	Word Form	Expanded Form
	three hundred fifty and seven hundredths	$(300) + (50) + \left(7 \times \frac{1}{100}\right)$
34.029		
	sixty and forty-three hundredths	
		$(700) + (20) + \left(8 \times \frac{1}{10}\right) +$ $\left(3 \times \frac{1}{1,000}\right)$

9.   510
       × 3

10.   1,981
        × 7

11.   34
        × 13

12.   982
        × 45

13. 6)580

14. 8)1,202

15. 12)492

16. 14)4,207

17.   8.1
       + 12.97

18.   297.8
        − 199

19.   673.4
        − 13.06

20.   626.707
        + 37.9

21. 4)$12.48

22.   88.6
        × 5

23.   0.2
        × 0.9

24. 9)561

Powers of 10

These cards can be used in a variety of ways to review and assess a student's understanding of working with powers of 10. There are 10 sets of matching cards with one card showing an expression (i.e., $10^3 \times 18.3$) and the other showing the product or quotient in standard form. Have a student match the card for a quick assessment. Or, have students play a memory game by displaying all of the cards facedown in an array and then taking turns flipping over two at a time until a match is made. You could also give each student a card and ask that students mingle to find their match.

0.008 A	$0.8 \div 10^2$ B
14×10^2 C	$10^2 \times 18$ D
64×10^4 E	$1,400$ F
$1,800$ G	$640,000$ H

0.019 **I**	0.837 **J**
100 **K**	0.001×10^5 **L**
6×10^3 **M**	$10^4 \times 6.1$ **N**
$19 \div 10^3$ **O**	$837 \div 10^3$ **P**
6,000 **Q**	61,000 **R**

Powers of 10

Solve.

1. $10^2 =$ _____

2. $10^3 =$ _____

3. $10^4 =$ _____

4. $10^5 =$ _____

5. $10^6 =$ _____

6. $10^7 =$ _____

Complete each pattern.

7. $4 \times$ _____ $= 16$

$4 \times$ _____ $= 160$

$4 \times$ _____ $= 1,600$

$4 \times$ _____ $= 16,000$

$4 \times$ _____ $= 160,000$

8. _____ $\times 8 = 72$

_____ $\times 8 = 720$

_____ $\times 8 = 7,200$

_____ $\times 8 = 72,000$

_____ $\times 8 = 720,000$

9. Rule: Multiply by 10

0.78, _____, _____, _____, _____

10. Rule: Divide by 10

8,320, _____, _____, _____, _____

11. Rule: Multiply by 10

0.06, _____, _____, _____, _____

12. Rule: Divide by 10

10,000, _____, _____, _____, _____

13. Rule: Multiply by 10

14.82, _____, _____, _____, _____

14. Rule: Divide by 10

6,200, _____, _____, _____, _____

Multiplying Whole Numbers

Solve.

1.   62
         × 7

2.   723
         × 6

3.   608
         × 4

4.   2,307
         ×   5

5.   34
         × 21

6.   72
         × 36

7.   129
         × 45

8.   2,321
         ×   68

9.   263
         × 145

10.   907
         × 265

11. 1,630
         ×   563

12. 1,422
         ×   512

13. 15 × 12 × 19 = _____

14. 348 × 13 × 63 = _____

Solve. Show your work.

15. Westburg Elementary purchased new science textbooks for all of its students. The books came in 42 boxes with 32 books in each box. How many science textbooks did the school purchase in all?

16. Stephanie poured 72 glasses of lemonade for the family reunion. If each glass holds 12 ounces, how much total lemonade did she pour?

17. A factory produces 690 boxes of crayons each hour. How many crayons would they produce in five hours if there are 24 crayons in each box?

Dividing Whole Numbers

Solve.

1. 6)678

2. 3)441

3. 9)846

4. 7)560

5. 4)833

6. 5)2,919

7. 8)5,034

8. 6)8,182

9. 15)690

10. 12)372

11. 14)2,835

12. 22)1,309

13. $1,800 \div 60 =$ _____

14. $8,100 \div 90 =$ _____

15. $3,600 \div 40 =$ _____

How do you know?

_____

_____

Solve. Show your work.

16. The music auditorium seats 1,260 people. Each row has 28 seats. How many rows are in the auditorium?

17. The restaurant used 3,468 eggs last month. The manager plans to order eggs for next month based on last month's usage. How many dozen eggs did the restaurant use last month?

18. Three hundred thirty-six participants signed up to run a 5K for a local charity fund-raiser. Runners lined up in rows of 12. How many rows of runners were there?

Name _____   Date _____

Multiplying and Dividing Whole Numbers

Solve.

1. 347 × 84 = _____

2. 684 ÷ 32 = _____

3. 368 ÷ 22 = _____

4. 49 × 86 = _____

5. 5,830 ÷ 55 = _____

6. 3,874 × 226 = _____

7. 589 × 741 = _____

8. 990 ÷ 36 = _____

Solve. Show your work.

9. The field trip to the museum cost $45 per student. If there were 68 students going, how much did the field trip cost altogether?

10. Eight members of the book club read the same book for last month's book study. If together they read a total of 1,728 pages, how many pages were in the book?

Reading, Writing, and Comparing Decimals

1. Complete the chart.

Standard Form	Word Form	Expanded Form
	eighty-seven and thirty-six hundredths	$(80) + (7) + \left(3 \times \frac{1}{10}\right) + \left(6 \times \frac{1}{100}\right)$
900.054		
	four and sixty-seven hundredths	
		$(700) + (20) + \left(7 \times \frac{1}{10}\right) + \left(2 \times \frac{1}{1,000}\right)$
	thirty-seven thousandths	
303.6		

Write each set in order from least to greatest.

2. 7.49, 7.05, 7.505, 7.55, 7.5

_____

3. 82.8, 88, 82.08, 88.8, 88.008

_____

4. 0.5, 0.05, 0.555, 0.505, 0.005

_____

Compare using **>**, **<**, or **=**.

5. 3.78 $\bigcirc$ 3.8

6. 4,500.8 $\bigcirc$ 4,500.789

7. 56.7 $\bigcirc$ 57.01

8. fourteen thousandths $\bigcirc$ one tenth

9. 0.1 $\bigcirc$ 0.017

10. sixteen hundredths $\bigcirc$ twenty-two thousandths

11. 45.6 $\bigcirc$ 45.345

12. 2,693.2 $\bigcirc$ 2,822.1

13. 22.02 $\bigcirc$ 22.2

14. five tenths $\bigcirc$ fifty hundredths

Rounding Decimals

Place each decimal on the number line. Then, round to the nearest whole number.

1. A. 0.6 _____   B. 0.40 _____   C. 0.2 _____   D. 0.80 _____

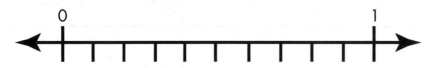

2. A. 14.1 _____   B. 15.60 _____   C. 15.25 _____   D. 14.9 _____

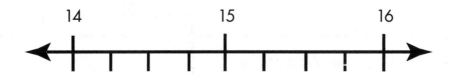

3. A. 33.33 _____   B. 33.8 _____   C. 32.8 _____   D. 32.99 _____

Round each number to the place of the underlined digit.

4. 4,670.<u>5</u>2 _____

5. 892.<u>3</u>3 _____

6. 0.<u>6</u>29 _____

7. 92<u>6</u>.099 _____

8. 4<u>2</u>.431 _____

9. 2<u>4</u>3.5 _____

10. 5.8<u>8</u>6 _____

11. 4.<u>3</u>47 _____

12. 0.6<u>2</u>9 _____

13. <u>1</u>.309 _____

14. Round 7.469 to the nearest

hundredth _____

tenth _____

whole number _____

15. Round 0.509 to the nearest

hundredth _____

tenth _____

whole number _____

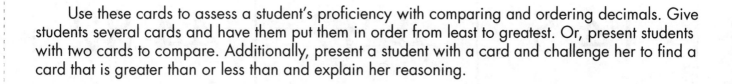

Use these cards to assess a student's proficiency with comparing and ordering decimals. Give students several cards and have them put them in order from least to greatest. Or, present students with two cards to compare. Additionally, present a student with a card and challenge her to find a card that is greater than or less than and explain her reasoning.

0.5	0.567	0.42
0.08	0.302	0.7
0.07	0.008	0.1

Comparing and Ordering Decimals

14.5	4.89	44.82
420.56	6.534	72.96
28.345	0.68	0.834
5.4	9.789	1.53

7.654	7.456	17.844
17.9	46.68	46.118
82.003	82.3	5.12
5.4	461.951	461.099

Name _____ Date _____

Adding and Subtracting Decimals

Solve.

1.   3.4
        + 6.8

2.   17.4
        + 0.6

3.   10.18
        + 0.88

4.   53.2
        + 12.7

5.   0.8
        − 0.4

6.   10.6
        − 6.6

7.   63.84
        − 25.55

8.   18.02
        − 9.63

9. 61.5 + 38.66 = _____

10. 1.06 − 0.38 = _____

11. 157.89 + 23.33 = _____

12. 50.1 − 10.74 = _____

Solve. Show your work.

13. Malia's twin sisters each weighed 6.6 pounds at birth. How much did her sisters weigh altogether?

14. Over the weekend, it rained a total of 4.67 inches. If it rained 2.33 inches on Saturday, how much did it rain on Sunday?

Name _____   Date _____

Multiplying and Dividing Decimals

Solve. Write quotients as decimals.

1.   8.4
       × 6

2.   5.8
       × 3

3.   64
       × 0.6

4.   39
       × 1.9

5. 5)667

6. 8)2,500

7. 6)2,529

8. 4)2,481

9.   7.04
       × 0.9

10. 4)12.48

11. $4.70
       × 1.2

12. 3)14.76

Solve. Show your work.

13. New York City received 33.6 inches of snow over a three-day period. What was the average amount of snowfall they received each day?

14. Kennan bought 2.5 pounds of grapes at the grocery store for $0.98 per pound. How much did Kennan spend on grapes?

Operations with Decimals

Solve. Write quotients as decimals.

1. 40.8 + 310.9

2. 8.2 × 4

3. 48 ÷ 1.2

4. 74.3 – 6.97

5. 0.3 × 0.8

6. 3,241.8 + 98.061

7. 100.8 – 73.47

8. 650 ÷ 0.8

Solve. Show your work.

9. The gardening club wants to plant a 3.9-acre field with pine trees. The first day they were able to plant 0.6 acres. If they continue at this rate, how many days will it take to plant the entire field?

10. A marathon is 26.219 miles long. If Dan ran 6 marathons last year, how many miles did he run in all?

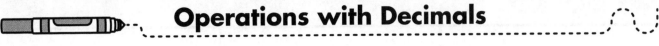

Operations with Decimals

Use these cards to assess a student's understanding of adding, subtracting, multiplying, and dividing decimals. Have a student solve the problem on a card or cards to show his proficiency. Or, choose several of these cards to be sorted without solving to assess a student's understanding. Students must have a solid grasp of number sense and place value to sort the cards into categories like "less than 1" and "more than 1."

0.58 + 0.4	0.099 + 0.4	0.6 + 0.6
A	**B**	**C**
0.59 + 0.5	3.5 – 2.88	67 – 66.021
D	**E**	**F**
127.05 – 125.99	5.03 – 4.003	0.07 + 0.106
G	**H**	**I**

0.5 × 0.3 **J**	0.81 × 0.2 **K**	1.8 ÷ 0.9 **L**
7.2 ÷ 9 **M**	3.5 ÷ 7 **N**	0.2 × 0.99 **O**
1.6 ÷ 2 **P**	0.4 × 0.32 **Q**	6 × 0.2 **R**
1 ÷ 0.8 **S**	10 × 0.1 **T**	0.42 × 0.4 **U**

A. Explain why 5.8 is greater than 5.599. Use words and/or pictures.

B. Write the following decimals in order from least to greatest.

0.365, 0.29, 0.4, 0.048, 0.39

_____ , _____ , _____ ,

_____ , _____

C. Write the number in both expanded form and word form.

4,502.304

_____

_____

_____

D. Draw a number line and place the decimals appropriately.

0.8, 0.25, 0.99, 0.501

E. Solve.

Kade bought a 3-pack of footballs for $9.99. How much did each football cost?

F. Solve.

Dawson purchased 4 packs of baseball cards, 6 packs of football cards, and 8 packs of basketball cards.
How much did Dawson spend? _____

Baseball cards	$1.49 per pack
Football cards	$0.89 per pack
Basketball cards	$1.19 per pack

G. Solve.

The social committee ordered 26 dozen roses for the upcoming banquet. Each dozen costs $7.89. How much did the committee spend on roses?

H. Solve.

Quincey divided 48 by a power of 10. He got the quotient 4.8. By what power of ten did Quincey divide? _____ Explain your answer.

_____

_____

Solve.

Noah's class of 28 students sits in groups of 8 at the cafeteria tables. How many cafeteria tables will Noah's class fill up completely? Explain your answer.

I

Solve.

Mischa's art class of 32 students collected plastic bottles for an art project. To complete the project, they need a total of 500 bottles. Each student brought in 16 bottles. Did they collect enough? Show your work.

J

Solve.

The nursery ordered 156 flats of petunias. Each flat contained 24 petunias. How many petunias did the nursery order in all?

K

Solve.

Tisha ordered the lunch special for $4.99, a drink for $1.49, and a slice of cake for $2.30. About how much did Tisha spend on lunch?

L

Solve.

Simone filled her car's gas tank with 14.6 gallons of gas. A gallon of gas cost $2.10. How much did Simone spend on gas?

M

Solve.

The Sanchez family drove 289.12 miles in 5.2 hours. On average, how many miles did they drive each hour?

N

Create your own pattern and rule similar to the one below.

Rule: Divide by 10.
        560, 56, 5.6, 0.56

Rule: _____

_____ , _____ , _____ , _____

O

Create your own pattern and rule similar to the one below.

Rule: Multiply by 10.
        0.89, 8.9, 89, 890

Rule: _____

_____ , _____ , _____ , _____

P

Name _____ Date _____

✦ Show What You Know ✦
Number and Operations—Fractions

1. Write the following fractions in order from least to greatest.

$\frac{2}{3}, \frac{5}{8}, \frac{1}{10}, \frac{6}{12}, \frac{1}{4}$ _____ , _____ , _____ , _____ , _____

2. Compare using **<**, **>**, or **=**.

$\frac{1}{12} \bigcirc \frac{1}{8}$ $\frac{2}{3} \bigcirc \frac{5}{6}$ $\frac{6}{10} \bigcirc \frac{4}{5}$

3. Rewrite each mixed number as an improper fraction.

$4\frac{1}{5}$ _____ $3\frac{6}{7}$ _____ $2\frac{3}{4}$ _____

4. Write each fraction in lowest terms.

$\frac{6}{10}$ _____ $\frac{2}{8}$ _____ $\frac{4}{20}$ _____

5. Place each fraction on the number line. Then, round to the nearest whole number.

A. $\frac{1}{2}$ _____   B. $\frac{3}{4}$ _____   C. $\frac{1}{8}$ _____   D. $\frac{11}{12}$ _____

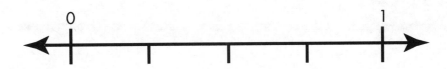

E. $2\frac{1}{3}$ _____   F. $\frac{7}{4}$ _____   G. $\frac{8}{12}$ _____   H. $\frac{12}{8}$ _____

6. Six friends are sharing 4 packs of baseball cards equally.

What fraction of a pack will each friend get? _____

Solve. Show your work. Reduce to lowest terms.

7. $\dfrac{3}{8} + \dfrac{4}{8} =$

8. $\dfrac{5}{6} - \dfrac{2}{6} =$

9. $\dfrac{4}{5} + \dfrac{2}{5} =$

10. $\dfrac{1}{2} + \dfrac{1}{6} =$

11. $\dfrac{3}{4} - \dfrac{3}{8} =$

12. $\dfrac{7}{8} + \dfrac{3}{4} =$

13. $4 \times \dfrac{3}{4} =$

14. $\dfrac{1}{4} \times \dfrac{1}{5} =$

15. $4 \times 3\dfrac{1}{2} =$

16. $1 \div \dfrac{1}{3} =$

17. $\dfrac{1}{4} \div 2 =$

18. $3 \div \dfrac{1}{2} =$

✦ Show What You Know ✦
Number and Operations—Fractions

1. Write the following fractions in order from least to greatest.

$\frac{5}{6}, \frac{1}{3}, \frac{1}{8}, \frac{3}{5}, \frac{3}{4}$ _____, _____, _____, _____, _____

2. Compare using **<**, **>**, or **=**.

$\frac{1}{6}$ ◯ $\frac{1}{8}$ $\frac{2}{3}$ ◯ $\frac{3}{4}$ $\frac{3}{10}$ ◯ $\frac{3}{5}$

3. Rewrite each improper fraction as a mixed number.

$\frac{6}{5}$ _____ $\frac{37}{6}$ _____ $\frac{20}{3}$ _____

4. Write each fraction in lowest terms.

$\frac{2}{6}$ _____ $\frac{25}{100}$ _____ $\frac{6}{9}$ _____

5. Place each fraction on the number line. Then, round to the nearest whole number.

A. $\frac{4}{5}$ _____   B. $\frac{1}{6}$ _____   C. $\frac{7}{10}$ _____   D. $\frac{25}{100}$ _____

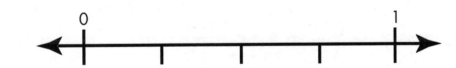

E. $1\frac{1}{10}$ _____   F. $\frac{13}{6}$ _____   G. $\frac{11}{4}$ _____   H. $\frac{10}{5}$ _____

6. Ten friends are sharing 4 bags of popcorn.

What fraction of a bag will each friend get? _____

Solve. Show your work. Reduce to lowest terms.

7. $\dfrac{3}{5} + \dfrac{2}{5} =$

8. $\dfrac{7}{8} - \dfrac{2}{8} =$

9. $\dfrac{5}{6} + \dfrac{5}{6} =$

10. $\dfrac{3}{4} + \dfrac{2}{3} =$

11. $\dfrac{8}{10} - \dfrac{1}{2} =$

12. $\dfrac{5}{6} + \dfrac{1}{3} =$

13. $2 \times \dfrac{1}{4} =$

14. $\dfrac{1}{3} \times \dfrac{1}{5} =$

15. $3 \times 2\dfrac{1}{3} =$

16. $2 \div \dfrac{1}{8} =$

17. $\dfrac{1}{2} \div 2 =$

18. $3 \div \dfrac{1}{4} =$

Use these cards to assess a student's proficiency with adding and subtracting fractions. Present a student with a card and have her solve the problem. If desired, have her support her answer with an explanation or model. You may also choose several cards to create a whole-class assessment. Or, assess number sense of fractions by having the student sort the cards into categories like *less than half*, *more than half*, or *greater than one* without solving.

$\dfrac{1}{8} + \dfrac{1}{2}$	$\dfrac{1}{2} + \dfrac{1}{4}$	$\dfrac{4}{5} - \dfrac{3}{10}$
A	**B**	**C**
$\dfrac{5}{6} + \dfrac{3}{12}$	$\dfrac{2}{3} + \dfrac{3}{4}$	$\dfrac{1}{6} + \dfrac{3}{8}$
D	**E**	**F**
$\dfrac{3}{8} + \dfrac{1}{2}$	$\dfrac{7}{8} - \dfrac{1}{2}$	$\dfrac{1}{2} - \dfrac{1}{6}$
G	**H**	**I**

$\dfrac{7}{10} - \dfrac{1}{2}$ **J**	$\dfrac{1}{12} + \dfrac{3}{6}$ **K**	$\dfrac{1}{4} + \dfrac{1}{8}$ **L**
$\dfrac{2}{3} - \dfrac{1}{6}$ **M**	$2\dfrac{1}{3} - 1\dfrac{7}{10}$ **N**	$1\dfrac{1}{4} + 2\dfrac{3}{8}$ **O**
$4\dfrac{1}{2} - 2\dfrac{2}{3}$ **P**	$3\dfrac{1}{2} + \dfrac{7}{8}$ **Q**	$5\dfrac{1}{3} - 2\dfrac{3}{4}$ **R**
$1\dfrac{2}{5} + 1\dfrac{3}{10}$ **S**	$1\dfrac{7}{8} - \dfrac{3}{4}$ **T**	$2\dfrac{4}{5} + 1\dfrac{1}{10}$ **U**

Name _____ Date _____

Adding and Subtracting Fractions

Solve.

1.  **+** 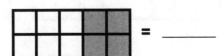 = _____

2.  **–** = _____

3. 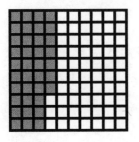 **+** 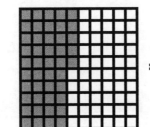 = _____

4. $\dfrac{1}{6}$
  $+\ \dfrac{2}{6}$
  _____

5. $\dfrac{3}{8}$
  $+\ \dfrac{6}{8}$
  _____

6. $\dfrac{3}{4}$
  $-\ \dfrac{1}{4}$
  _____

7. $\dfrac{28}{100}$
  $-\ \dfrac{13}{100}$
  _____

8. $\dfrac{1}{8}$
  $+\ \dfrac{1}{2}$
  _____

9. $\dfrac{1}{2}$
  $-\ \dfrac{1}{3}$
  _____

10. $\dfrac{3}{5}$
  $+\ \dfrac{3}{10}$
  _____

11. $\dfrac{7}{12}$
  $-\ \dfrac{1}{2}$
  _____

Write the missing number to make each equation true.

12. $\dfrac{}{16} + \dfrac{1}{16} = \dfrac{1}{2}$

13. $\dfrac{5}{9} - \dfrac{}{9} = \dfrac{4}{9}$

14. $\dfrac{7}{10} - \dfrac{3}{10} = \dfrac{}{5}$

15. $\dfrac{1}{4} + \dfrac{1}{4} = \dfrac{}{1}$

Name _____ Date _____

Multiplying Fractions

Use the model to complete each equation.

1. $5 \times \dfrac{}{3} = —$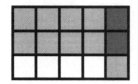

2. $\dfrac{1}{5} \times \dfrac{2}{3} = —$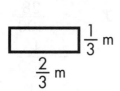

3. $— \times \dfrac{3}{5} = \dfrac{3}{10}$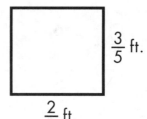

Find each product. Show your work.

4. $2 \times \dfrac{2}{3} =$

5. $\dfrac{4}{9} \times 3 =$

6. $5\dfrac{1}{2} \times \dfrac{3}{5} =$

Find the area of each figure.

$\dfrac{1}{3}$ m
$\dfrac{2}{3}$ m

$\dfrac{3}{5}$ ft.
$\dfrac{2}{3}$ ft.

$\dfrac{2}{5}$ yd.
$\dfrac{3}{4}$ yd.

7. A = _____

8. A = _____

9. A = _____

Solve. Show your work.

10. Jay ran 4 laps around the track. Each lap is $1\dfrac{1}{3}$ mile. How many miles did Jay run?

11. The class bought 8 packs of clay for an art project. They used $\dfrac{2}{3}$ of each pack. How many packs of clay do they have left?

12. Mia has $\dfrac{3}{5}$ of the cake left over after the party. She gives $\dfrac{1}{2}$ of what is left to her cousin. What portion of the whole cake did her cousin get? Draw a model to show your answer.

Use these cards to assess a student's understanding of multiplying fractions. Present a student with a card and have her solve the problem. If desired, have her support her answer with an explanation or model. You may also choose several cards to create a whole-class assessment. Or, assess number sense of fractions by having the student sort the cards into categories like *less than one* and *more than one* without solving.

$3 \times \dfrac{1}{7}$	$\dfrac{1}{4} \times \dfrac{1}{3}$	$\dfrac{1}{2} \times \dfrac{1}{4}$
A	**B**	**C**
$\dfrac{3}{4} \times 5$	$4 \times \dfrac{1}{3}$	$\dfrac{1}{5} \times \dfrac{2}{3}$
D	**E**	**F**
$\dfrac{3}{7} \times \dfrac{1}{2}$	$10 \times \dfrac{4}{5}$	$\dfrac{1}{2} \times 5$
G	**H**	**I**

$\dfrac{5}{6} \times \dfrac{2}{3}$	$\dfrac{5}{8} \times \dfrac{1}{2}$	$\dfrac{3}{5} \times 4$
J	**K**	**L**
$3 \times \dfrac{5}{8}$	$\dfrac{3}{8} \times \dfrac{1}{3}$	$\dfrac{3}{10} \times \dfrac{2}{3}$
M	**N**	**O**
$\dfrac{7}{8} \times 3$	$\dfrac{1}{5} \times 4$	$\dfrac{3}{4} \times 6$
P	**Q**	**R**
$\dfrac{1}{2} \times \dfrac{5}{6}$	$\dfrac{2}{5} \times \dfrac{1}{2}$	$\dfrac{4}{5} \times \dfrac{1}{3}$
S	**T**	**U**

Name _____ Date _____

Multiplication as Scaling

Compare using **<**, **>**, or **=**.

1. $\frac{1}{2} \times \frac{3}{4}$ ◯ $\frac{3}{4}$

2. 4 ◯ $\frac{1}{6} \times 4$

3. $2 \times \frac{7}{8}$ ◯ 2

4. $\frac{5}{6} \times 5$ ◯ 5

5. $\frac{4}{4} \times \frac{3}{5}$ ◯ $\frac{3}{5}$

6. $2 \times \frac{5}{4}$ ◯ $\frac{5}{4}$

7. Which expression has a product greater than $\frac{3}{4}$?

◯ $\frac{1}{4} \times \frac{3}{4}$ ◯ $\frac{6}{6} \times \frac{3}{4}$

◯ $\frac{1}{2} \times \frac{3}{4}$ ◯ $2 \times \frac{3}{4}$

8. Which expression has a product less than $\frac{2}{3}$?

◯ $3 \times \frac{2}{3}$ ◯ $\frac{3}{3} \times \frac{2}{3}$

◯ $\frac{1}{4} \times \frac{2}{3}$ ◯ $\frac{3}{2} \times \frac{2}{3}$

9. Which expression has a product equal to $\frac{7}{5}$?

◯ $4 \times \frac{7}{5}$ ◯ $\frac{7}{4} \times \frac{7}{5}$

◯ $\frac{5}{5} \times \frac{7}{5}$ ◯ $\frac{1}{3} \times \frac{7}{5}$

10. How will the product $1\frac{2}{3} \times \frac{7}{8}$ compare to $1\frac{2}{3}$?

◯ It will be equal since the other factor is less than 1.

◯ There is not enough information to answer the question.

◯ It will be less since the other factor is less than 1.

◯ It will be greater since the other factor is less than 1.

Fractions as Division

1. $4 \div 3 = \dfrac{4}{}$ **2.** _____ $\div\, 5 = \dfrac{9}{5}$

3. Draw a model or number line showing $7 \div 4 = \dfrac{7}{4}$.

4. Draw a model or number line showing $5 \div 2 = \dfrac{5}{2}$.

Solve. Show your work.

5. Six friends want to share 2 cookies. How much will each friend get?

6. After lunch, 8 students want to share 6 candy bars equally. How much will each student get?

7. The class is given 12 minutes to complete 10 math problems. How much time do they have to spend on each problem?

8. Bailey and her two sisters are allowed to play video games for two hours over the weekend if they share the controller equally. How long will each child have the controller?

Dividing Fractions

1. Draw a model to represent $2 \div \frac{1}{3}$.

2. Draw a model to represent $\frac{1}{4} \div 3$.

3. If 4 friends share 5 candy bars equally, what part of a candy bar does each friend get?

_____

Write the division problem that you would use to solve this problem. _____

Write the division problem as a fraction. _____

Solve. Show your work.

4. Tyesha had $\frac{1}{2}$ of a sub sandwich left over after yesterday's picnic. She plans to divide it equally between herself and her two brothers. How much of the original sub sandwich will they each get?

5. Sam purchased 5 pounds of hamburger meat for a cookout. How many burgers can he make if he plans to make $\frac{1}{3}$ -pound burgers?

6. William bought 8 ounces of chocolate truffles. Each truffle was $\frac{1}{4}$ ounce. How many truffles did he buy? Show your work.

Name _____ Date _____

Fraction Word Problems

Solve. Show your work.

1. The groundskeeper and his helper each mowed $\frac{3}{8}$ of the field before dark. How much do they have left to mow tomorrow?

2. After choosing a new paint color for their room, Sierra and Samantha painted for three hours on Saturday. Sierra painted $\frac{1}{4}$ of the room and Samantha painted $\frac{1}{3}$. How much more do they have left to paint?

3. Isabel mixed up 6 cups of cake batter. If Isabel used $\frac{1}{4}$ cup of batter to make each muffin, how many muffins can she make?

4. Noah had $\frac{3}{4}$ bag of popcorn left after the movie. If his brother ate $\frac{1}{2}$ of what was left over, what fraction of the whole bag did his brother eat?

5. Morgan is knitting a blanket. She finished $\frac{1}{5}$ of it on Monday and $\frac{1}{4}$ on Wednesday. How much more does Morgan have to knit before her blanket is complete?

Prove that $7 \div 2 = \frac{7}{2}$. Use words and/or pictures.

A

List three fractions equivalent to $\frac{1}{3}$. Explain how you know they are equivalent using words and/or pictures.

_____ , _____ , _____

B

Write the fractions in order from least to greatest.

$$\frac{4}{5}, \frac{25}{100}, \frac{1}{2}, \frac{1}{5}, \frac{3}{4}$$

_____ , _____ , _____ , _____ , _____

C

Complete the table.

Rule: Multiply by $\frac{1}{2}$.

In	8	2	$\frac{1}{2}$	$\frac{1}{4}$
Out				

D

Explain how you know $\frac{1}{2} \times \frac{1}{3} < \frac{1}{2}$. Use words and/or pictures.

E

Solve.

The Lee family rode bikes for $3\frac{2}{3}$ miles before lunch and $4\frac{1}{4}$ miles after lunch. How many miles did the Lee family ride in all?

F

Solve.

Lamar completed $\frac{1}{4}$ of his project at school and $\frac{2}{5}$ of his project at home over the weekend. How much more does he have left to complete?

G

Solve.

Kami purchased $3\frac{1}{2}$ yards of ribbon to make bows. If each bow takes $\frac{1}{4}$ yard of ribbon to make, how many bows can she make?

H

Solve.

Danielle ran $\frac{2}{3}$ of each lap at the track and walked the remainder of each lap. If she did 6 laps in all, how much did she run?

I

Solve.

Elijah and his three friends are planning to share three brownies evenly. What fraction of a brownie will each person get?

J

Solve.

Charlotte was $\frac{1}{2}$ of the way toward meeting her yearly reading goal in March. She achieved $\frac{1}{5}$ more of her reading goal by reading books over spring break. What part of the goal is left for Charlotte to meet?

K

Solve.

Maria planted an herb garden that measured $3\frac{1}{3}$ yards × 4 yards. What is the total area of Maria's garden?

L

Draw a number line and place the following fractions appropriately.

$$\frac{3}{4}, \frac{3}{12}, \frac{5}{4}$$

M

Draw an area model to represent the expression. Then, solve.

$$\frac{1}{3} \times \frac{1}{5} = \text{---}$$

N

Draw a model to represent the following expression. Then, solve.

$$\frac{4}{5} \times \frac{1}{2} = \text{---}$$

O

What time will it be in $3\frac{1}{4}$ hours? _____

P

Name _____ Date _____

✦ Show What You Know ✦
Measurement and Data

Compare using **<**, **>**, or **=**.

1. 4 yards ◯ 12 feet   **2.** 540 seconds ◯ 8 minutes   **3.** 2,250 pounds ◯ 1 ton

4. 1,000 grams = _____ kilogram

5. 6 pints = _____ cups

6. 3,000 milliliters = _____ liters

Write the measurements in order from least to greatest.

7. 5 m, 5 cm, 5 mm   _____, _____, _____

8. 5 yd., 12 ft., 130 in.   _____, _____, _____

9. 3 hr., 170 min., 9,000 sec.   _____, _____, _____

10. 30 cups, 2 gal., 13 pt., 5 qt. _____, _____, _____, _____

Jessi charted the lengths of her runs over the last two weeks. Use the line plot to answer
the questions.

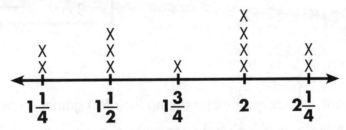

Distance Run (mi.)

11. How many times did Jessi run in the last two weeks? _____

12. How many total miles did Jessi run over the last two weeks? _____

13. What is the most common length of her runs? _____

14. On how many days did she run 2 miles or more? _____

Find the volume.

15. Count the cubes to find the length, width, and height of the prism.

l = _____ w = _____ h = _____

V = _____ cubic units

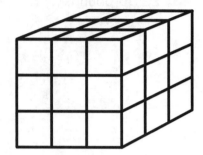

16. V = _____

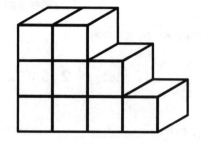

17. V = _____

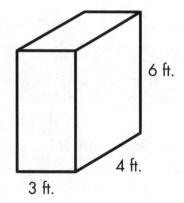

6 ft.

4 ft.

3 ft.

18. V = _____

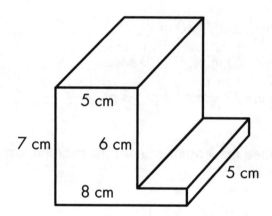

5 cm

7 cm   6 cm

8 cm   5 cm

Solve. Show your work.

19. The soccer team drank $1\frac{1}{2}$ cases of water during their last game. If each case of water had 24 bottles and each bottle held 2 pints, how many gallons of water did they drink at the game?

_____

20. If a cube has a side length of 4 feet, what is the total volume of the cube?

_____

Name _____ Date _____

✦ Show What You Know ✦
Measurement and Data

Compare using **<**, **>**, or **=**.

1. 6 quarts ◯ 2 gallons   **2.** 600 grams ◯ 6 kilograms   **3.** 8 yards ◯ 22 feet

4. 7 liters = _____ milliliters

5. 160 ounces = _____ pounds

6. 3,000 meters = _____ kilometers

Write the measurements in order from least to greatest.

7. 4 yd., 4 in., 4 mi., 4 ft.   _____ , _____ , _____ , _____

8. 5 qt., 15 cups, 1 gal., 6 pt.   _____ , _____ , _____ , _____

9. 1 km, 1,200 m, 1,000 mm   _____ , _____ , _____

10. 3,500 sec., 80 min., 1 hr.   _____ , _____ , _____

The line plot shows Seattle's rainfall last week. Use the line plot to answer the questions.

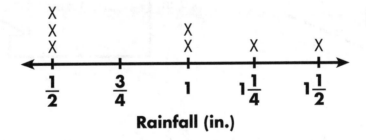

Rainfall (in.)

11. What was the total rainfall last week in Seattle? _____

12. How many days did it rain an inch or more? _____

13. What was the most common rainfall amount last week? _____

14. How many days did it rain $\frac{1}{2}$ inch? _____

Find the volume.

15. Count the cubes to find the length, width, and height of the prism.

l = _____ w = _____ h= _____

V = _____ cubic units

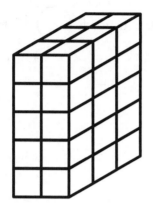

16. V = _____

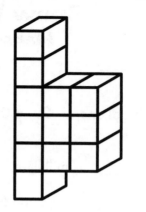

17. V = _____

7 in.

4 in.

4 in.

18. V = _____

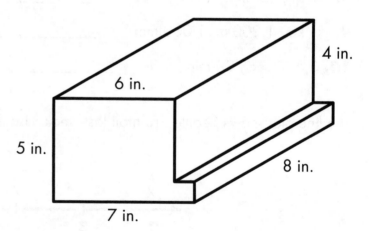

4 in.

6 in.

5 in.

8 in.

7 in.

Solve. Show your work.

19. On Jan's first drive, she hit the golf ball 48 yards. She then hit the ball 15 feet to reach the green. From there, she putted 18 inches to the hole. How many total inches did the ball travel?

20. If a cube has a side length of 8 inches, what is the total volume of the cube?

Measurement Conversions

Use these cards to assess basic understanding of measurement conversions. Have a student match equivalent measures, sort by what is being measured, and/or compare two or more measurements. You can also ask a student to give a measurement equivalent to the chosen card. Or, have students choose a matching set of cards and use it to create a table of equivalent measures. For example, if the student chooses cards B and H, he can complete a table showing how many inches are in 1, 2, 3, and 4 yards.

1 lb. **A**	1 yd. **B**	16 fl. oz. **C**	16 oz. **D**
2 cups **E**	240 min. **F**	27 ft. **G**	36 in. **H**
4 hr. **I**	4 qt. **J**	7 m **K**	700 cm **L**
8 kg **M**	8 pt. **N**	8,000 g **O**	9 yd. **P**

1 gal.	1 mi.	1 T.	18 ft.
Q	R	S	T
180 min.	2 qt.	2 yd.	2,000 lb.
U	V	W	X
3 hr.	32 fl. oz.	4 cups	4 pt.
Y	Z	AA	AB
5,280 ft.	5.5 m	550 cm	6 kg
AC	AD	AE	AF
6 yd.	6,000 g	72 in.	16 cups
AG	AH	AI	AJ

Name _____ Date _____

Measurement Conversions

Complete each sentence.

1. 1 milliliter is 1,000 times less liquid than 1 _____.

2. 1 quart is _____ times more liquid than 1 pint.

3. 1 meter is 1,000 times shorter than 1 _____.

4. 1 minute is _____ times as long as 1 second.

Complete each table.

5.

Pints	Quarts
2	
6	
	8
20	
	13

6.

Pounds	Tons
6,000	
12,000	
	7
	12
	20

7.

Kilometers	Meters
1	
	4,000
7	
	9,000
	15,000

Write the measurements in the spaces to make each scale true.

8. 3 kg, 3,600 g

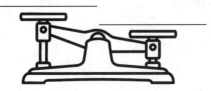

9. 3 tons, 5,500 pounds

10. Denise tracked how much water her dog drank each day for a week.

Mon.	Tues.	Wed.	Thur.	Fri.	Sat.	Sun.
450 mL	224 mL	547 mL	489 mL	510 mL	378 mL	502 mL

How many total liters did her dog drink in a week?

A. 0.31 liters   B. 31 liters

C. 3.1 liters   D. 310 liters

Interpreting Line Plots

Use the line plot to answer questions 1–3.

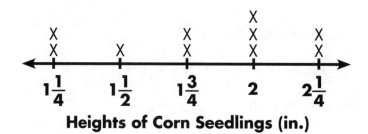

Heights of Corn Seedlings (in.)

1. How many seedlings were measured in all? _____

2. How many seedlings are exactly 2 inches tall? _____

3. How many seedlings are less than 2 inches tall? _____

Use the line plot to answer questions 4–7.

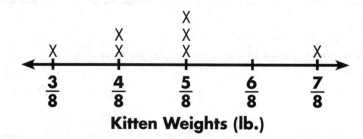

Kitten Weights (lb.)

4. How many total kittens are there? _____

5. What is the most common kitten weight? _____

6. What is the difference in weight between the heaviest and lightest kitten? _____

7. What is the total weight of all the kittens? _____

Line Plots

1. Create a line plot using the data.

Pumpkin Weights (lb.)

$6\frac{1}{2}$, $5\frac{3}{4}$, 6, $6\frac{1}{4}$, $5\frac{3}{4}$, $5\frac{3}{4}$, $6\frac{3}{4}$, $6\frac{1}{4}$, 6, $5\frac{3}{4}$

Use your line plot to answer questions 2–7.

2. The lightest pumpkin weighs _____ .

The heaviest pumpkin weighs _____ .

3. What is the difference between the weights of the heaviest and the lightest pumpkins?

_____

4. How many total pumpkins are represented in the line plot? _____

5. How much do the pumpkins weigh altogether? _____

6. The most common pumpkin weight for this batch of pumpkins is _____ .

7. How many pumpkins weigh more than 6 pounds? _____

How do you know?

_____

_____

_____

Understanding Volume

Circle the prism with the largest volume in each set.

1.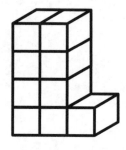

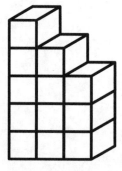

2.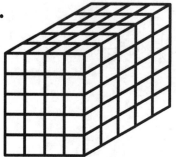

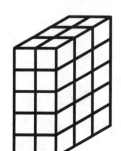

3.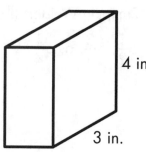

4 in.

3 in.

2 in.

3 in.

3 in.

2 in.

Count the cubes to find the volume.

4. V = _____ cubic units

5. l = _____ w = _____ h = _____

V = _____ cubic units

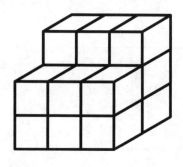

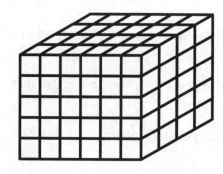

6. Explain the difference between 12 square units and 12 cubic units.

_____

_____

_____

Finding Volume

Find the volume.

1. V = _____ cubic units

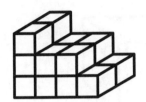

2. V = _____ cubic units

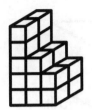

3. V = _____ cubic units

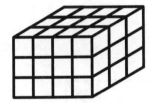

l = _____   w = _____   h = _____

4. V = _____ cubic units

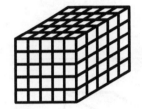

l = _____   w = _____   h = _____

5. V = _____ cubic units

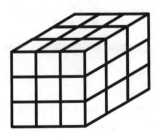

6. V = _____ cubic units

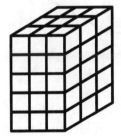

7. Use the prisms to explain how unit cubes and the dimensions are related to finding volume.

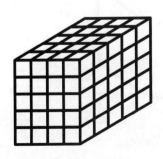

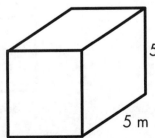

5 m

5 m

4 m

_____

_____

_____

_____

Finding Volume with a Formula

Find the volume.

1. V = _____

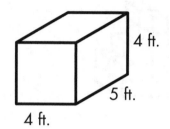

4 ft.
5 ft.
4 ft.

2. V = _____

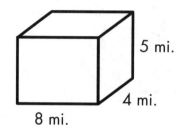

5 mi.
4 mi.
8 mi.

3. V = _____

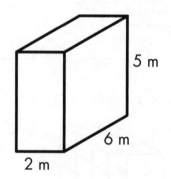

5 m
6 m
2 m

4. V = _____

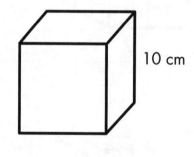

10 cm

5. If the total volume of the prism below is 96 cubic miles, find the missing measurement. Show your work.

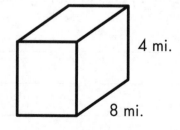

4 mi.
8 mi.

_____

6. If the total volume of the prism below is 144 cubic meters, find the missing measurement. Show your work.

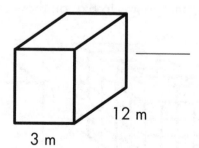

_____

12 m
3 m

Volume of Composite Figures

Find the total volume of each figure.

1. V = _____

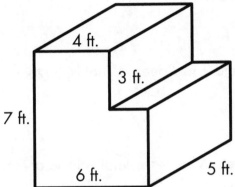

4 ft.

3 ft.

7 ft.

6 ft.

5 ft.

2. V = _____

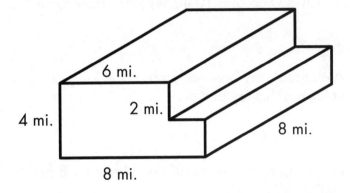

6 mi.

2 mi.

4 mi.

8 mi.

8 mi.

3. V = _____

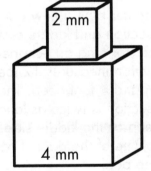

2 mm

4 mm

4. V = _____

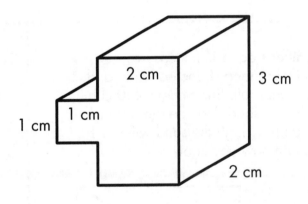

2 cm

3 cm

1 cm

1 cm

2 cm

5. V = _____

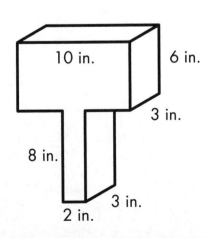

10 in.

6 in.

3 in.

8 in.

3 in.

2 in.

6. V = _____

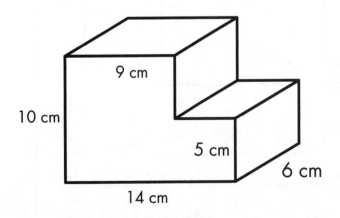

9 cm

10 cm

5 cm

6 cm

14 cm

Volume Word Problems

Solve. Show your work.

1. Caden played with 1-inch cubed wooden blocks. When it was time to clean up, Caden neatly placed all 250 blocks in a box without any gaps or overlaps. The box measured 5 inches wide and 10 inches long. How tall is Caden's box?

2. Alejandro's toy box measures 3 feet long, 2 feet wide, and 2 feet deep. What is the total volume of his toy box?

3. A moving container measures 12 feet by 8 feet by 10 feet. What is the total volume of the container?

---

4. Heather's aquarium measures 15 inches long, 8 inches wide, and 10 inches tall. She bought 240 cubic inches of sand. Use the diagram to shade how high the sand will reach. Explain how you know.

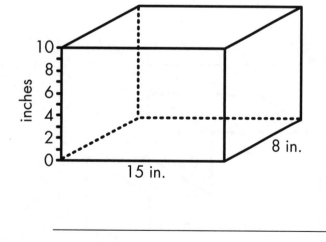

15 in.   8 in.

_____

_____

_____

5. The aquatic center built a new pool. The competition section and kiddie section are connected, forming an L-shaped pool. The kiddie section measures 12 feet long, 12 feet wide, and 4 feet deep. The competition section is twice as long, wide, and deep as the kiddie side. What is the total volume of the pool? Draw a diagram of the pool.

Find the volume.

V = _____

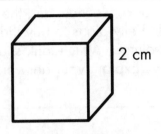

2 cm

A

The rectangular prism has a volume of 60 cubic feet. Find the missing measurement.

_____

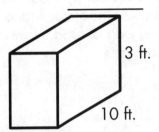

3 ft.

10 ft.

B

Solve.

1 L – 120 mL = _____ mL

3 L + 220 mL = _____ mL

_____ mL – 2 L = 1,450 mL

C

Solve.

3,000 m + 4,000 m = _____ km

4 km – 2,200 m = _____ m

3,000 m – 1.5 km = _____ m

D

Solve.

5 lb. – 20 oz. = _____ oz.

38 oz. – 1 lb. = _____ oz.

3 lb. + _____ oz. = 54 oz.

E

How many grams are equivalent to

55 kilograms? _____

How many kilograms are equivalent to

6,600 grams? _____

How many grams are equivalent to

100 kilograms? _____

F

Solve.

40 cm + 6 m = _____ cm

4.5 m + 200 cm = _____ cm

_____ m + 250 cm = 8 m

G

Solve.

4 gal. – 7 qt. = _____ qt.

16 qt. + 3 gal. = _____ gal.

2.5 gal. – 6 qt. = _____ qt.

H

Solve.

Mario feeds his puppy 6 ounces of food twice a day. At the store, Mario bought a three-pound bag of food. How many days will the bag last?

I

Kelly looks at two fish tanks. Tank A's base measures 12 inches by 14 inches, and the tank is 20 inches tall. Tank B's base measures 10 inches by 15 inches, and the tank is 22 inches tall. Kelly plans to buy the tank with the most volume. Which tank should she buy? Why? Explain your answer.

_____

_____

J

Solve.

Samaria makes lemonade to sell at the festival. She sold 64 cups of lemonade in all. How many gallons did she sell?

K

Draw a diagram to solve. Show your work.

What could be the dimensions of a rectangular prism with a volume of 60 cubic feet?

L

Solve.

Tony built two raised garden beds. The base of the first bed measured 5 feet by 5 feet, and the bed is 1 foot tall. The base of the second bed measured 6 feet by 4 feet, and the bed is also 1 foot tall. Which bed will hold the most soil?

M

Solve.

The box of crackers is 6 inches long, 2 inches wide, and 8 inches high. What is the volume of the cracker box?

N

Create a line plot using the data.

Backpack Weights (lb.)

$4\frac{3}{4}$, $5\frac{1}{4}$, 6, $5\frac{3}{4}$, $4\frac{3}{4}$, 5, $5\frac{1}{2}$, 6, $4\frac{3}{4}$, $5\frac{1}{2}$

O

Create a line plot using the data.

Worm Lengths (in.)

2, $1\frac{1}{2}$, $2\frac{1}{2}$, $1\frac{1}{2}$, 2, $2\frac{1}{4}$, $1\frac{1}{2}$, 2, $2\frac{1}{4}$, $1\frac{1}{2}$

P

Name _____   Date _____

✦ Show What You Know ✦
Geometry

1. Plot each point on the coordinate grid.

A (3, 5)
B (1, 4)
C (0, 7)
D (7, 2)

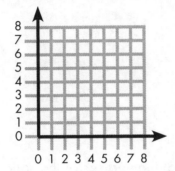

2. Record the ordered pairs that are located at the vertices of the square.

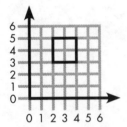

(_____ , _____)   (_____ , _____)

(_____ , _____)   (_____ , _____)

3. Draw a shape or figure that would not be considered a polygon.
Explain why it is not a polygon.

_____

_____

_____

4. Squares are members of all of the following groups except _____.

quadrilaterals   parallelograms   trapezoids   rectangles

5. Name two quadrilaterals that have four right angles. Draw them.

_____   _____

Name _____   Date _____

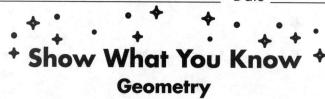

✦ Show What You Know ✦
Geometry

1. Plot each point on the coordinate grid.

A (4, 4)
B (6, 2)
C (1, 6)
D (3, 5)

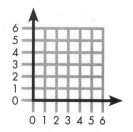

2. Record the ordered pairs that are located at the vertices of the square.

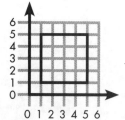

(_____ , _____)   (_____ , _____)

(_____ , _____)   (_____ , _____)

3. Draw a shape or figure that would not be considered a parallelogram. Explain why it is not a parallelogram.

_____

_____

_____

4. All of the following are quadrilaterals except for _____ .

    rectangles   squares   rhombuses   pentagons

5. Name two quadrilaterals that have two sets of parallel sides. Draw them.

_____   _____

Name _____ Date _____

Coordinate Planes

Use the coordinate grid to answer questions 1–4.

1. Which point is located at the origin? _____

2. Which point is located at (4, 1)? _____

3. Points *A*, *B*, *C*, and *D* form the vertices of what polygon?

_____

4. What are the coordinates of point *D*? _____

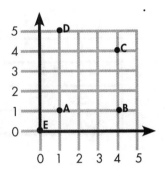

---

5. Plot the points on the coordinate plane.

A (2, 3)

B (3, 2)

C (5, 5)

D (1, 4)

E (0, 0)

6. Identify the points on the graph.

A = _____

B = _____

C = _____

D = _____

E = _____

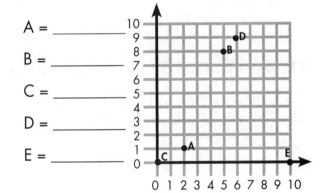

7. Add the ordered pair that completes the rectangle.

(2, 8)

(6, 8)

(6, 2)

_____

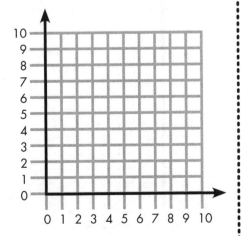

8. Wendy plotted the following three points on the coordinate plane. If she connected her points, what type of triangle did she plot?

(1, 7)

(4, 1)

(1, 1)

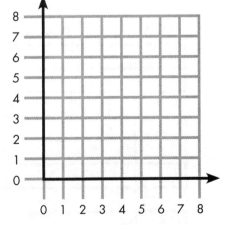

9. Hailey is tracking the growth of the sunflower she planted. If the plant continues to grow at the same rate, how tall will Hailey's sunflower be at week 6? Graph the results.

_____

Week	Height (in.)	Ordered Pair
1	2	(1, 2)
2	4	(2, 4)
3	6	(3, 6)
4	8	(4, 8)

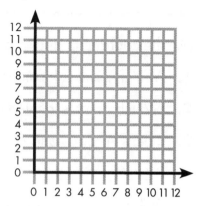

Use the coordinate plane to answer questions 10 and 11.

10. Daniel's house is located at (2, 8). Whose house is closest to Daniel?

_____

11. Reese lives two units west and three units north of Davis.

What are the coordinates of Reese's house? _____
Plot and label Reese's house on the grid.

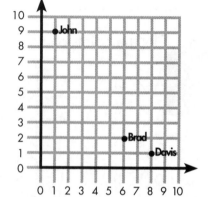

12. Rachel earns $2 every week for chores. If she saves her money, how much money will she have in 8 weeks?

_____

Complete the chart and plot the ordered pairs.

Week	Money Earned	Ordered Pair
1	2	(1, 2)
2		
3		
4		
5		
6		
7		
8		

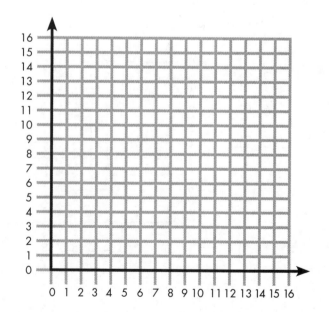

Two-Dimensional Figures

1. Complete the chart.

Polygon	Sides	Angles
triangle	3	3
octagon		
pentagon		
quadrilateral		
hexagon		

2. Draw and label the quadrilateral that has four congruent sides and no right angles.

_____

Use the diagram to answer questions 3–7.

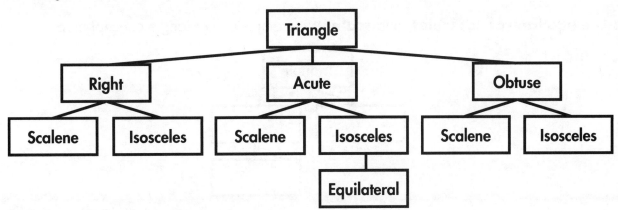

Circle **True** or **False** for each statement.

3. True False   A right triangle can also be an equilateral triangle.

4. True False   An acute triangle cannot be an equilateral triangle.

5. True False   An obtuse triangle can also be an equilateral triangle.

6. True False   A right triangle can also be an equilateral triangle.

7. True False   An obtuse triangle can also be an isosceles triangle.

8. Explain why all squares are rectangles but not all rectangles are squares.

_____

_____

Use the diagram to answer questions 9–12.

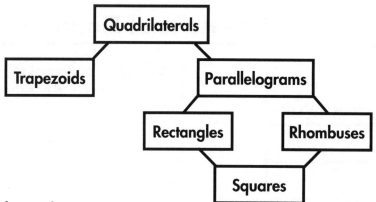

Circle **True** or **False** for each statement.

9. True   False   All parallelograms are quadrilaterals.

10. True   False   Trapezoids can also be rectangles.

11. True   False   A rhombus can also be a square.

12. True   False   All rectangles are parallelograms.

13. Use **equilateral**, **isosceles**, and **scalene** to complete the triangle concept map.

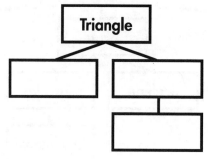

14. Draw an example of each type of polygon.

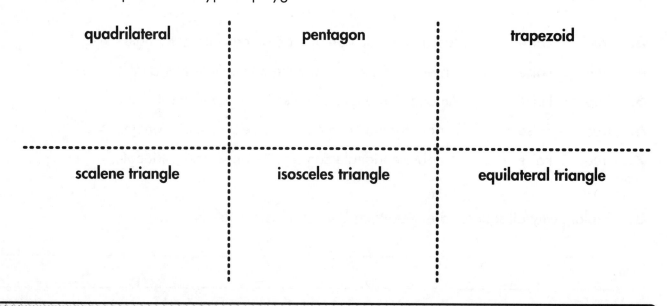

quadrilateral	pentagon	trapezoid
scalene triangle	isosceles triangle	equilateral triangle

Two-Dimensional Figures

Use these cards to assess a student's basic understanding of two-dimensional figures and their attributes. Have a student sort the cards by attributes or create hierarchies based on shape properties. Or, have students partner up and try to guess what shape the other has by describing its attributes.

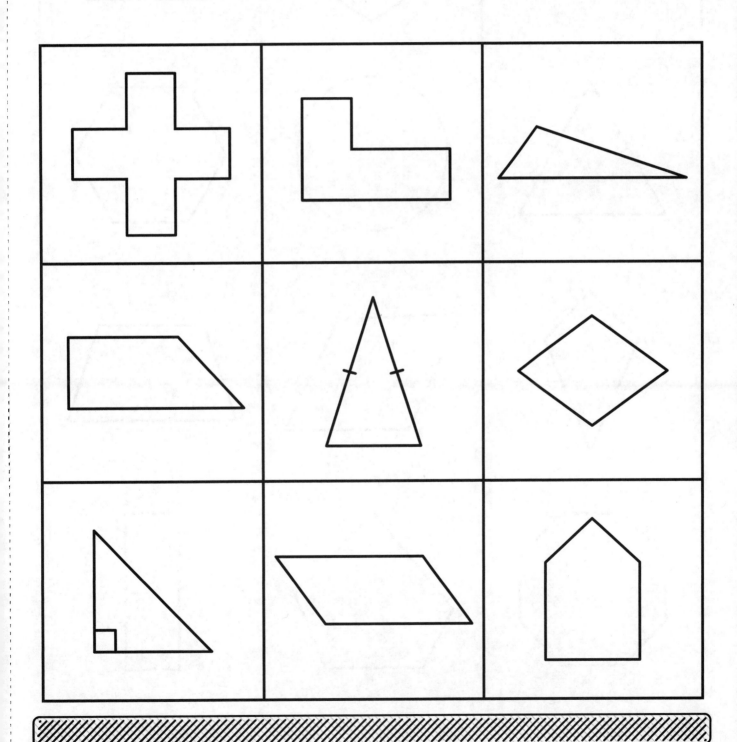

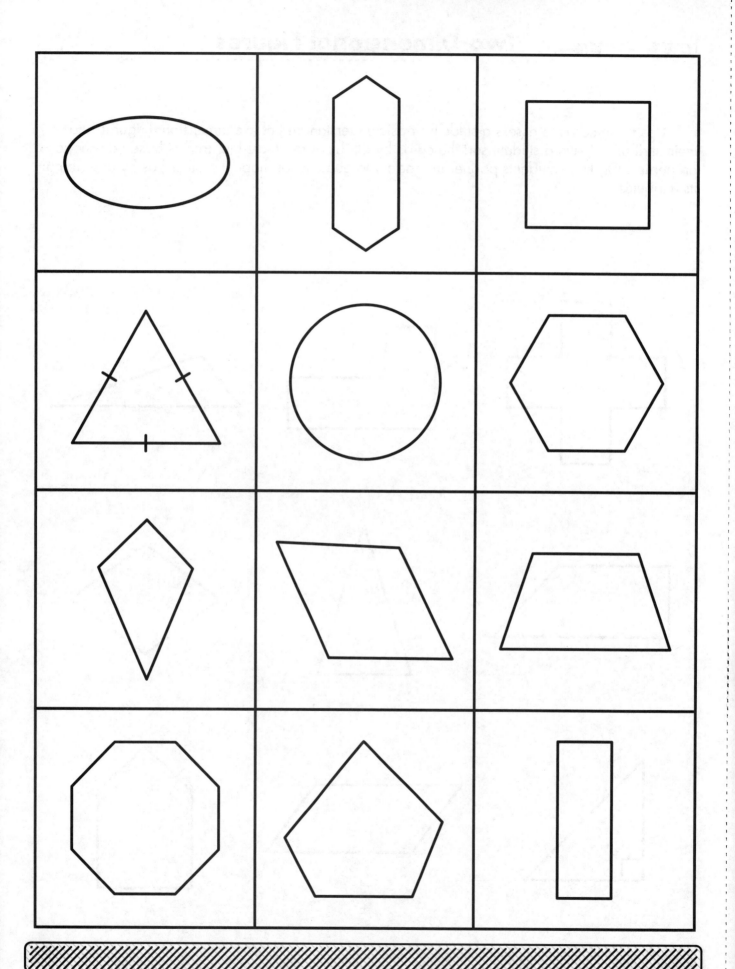

A

Draw a coordinate plane. Label the *x*-axis, the *y*-axis, and the origin.

B

Explain the difference in plotting the ordered pairs (3, 5) and (5, 3).

_____

_____

_____

_____

C

Renee's house is located at (4, 5) on the map. If her sister's house is located four units north, at what ordered pair is her sister's house?

(_____ , _____)

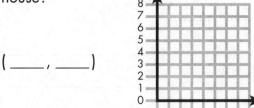

D

The flagpole is located at (3, 4). The water fountain is located two units east and three units north. Where is the water fountain located?

(_____ , _____)

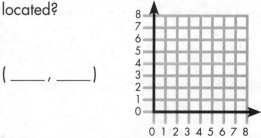

E

Brian graphed the following ordered pairs on a coordinate plane: (2, 5), (5, 7), (8, 5). Name the ordered pair that would complete the rhombus.

(_____ , _____)

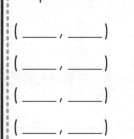

F

Plot four points on a coordinate grid to create a square. List the ordered pairs you used.

(_____ , _____)

(_____ , _____)

(_____ , _____)

(_____ , _____)

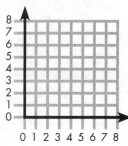

G

What type of triangle will the following ordered pairs create on a coordinate plane?

(1, 3)

(4, 3)

(4, 8)

_____

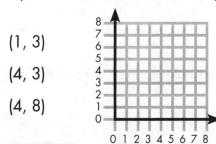

H

Draw and label an obtuse angle, acute angle, and right angle.

Name two parallograms that have have four right angles. Then, draw them.

_____

_____

I

Explain why a trapezoid is a quadrilateral but not a parallelogram.

_____

_____

_____

_____

J

Name two quadrilaterals that have four right angles. Draw them.

_____   _____

K

All rectangles are parallelograms.

True   **False**

Explain your answer.

_____

_____

_____

L

Draw and label a regular hexagon and an irregular hexagon. Explain the difference.

_____

_____

M

Draw a parallelogram with four right angles and four equal sides. What shape did you draw?

_____

N

List one attribute that squares and rectangles have in common.

_____

What makes them different?

_____

_____

O

What attribute do squares and rhombuses have in common?

_____

What attribute do they not share?

_____

_____

P

Answer Key

Pages 11–12

1. $11 \times (4 + 3)$; 2. 2; 3. $a < b$; 4. 12, 15, 18, Add 3; 6.1, 7.1, 8.1, Add 1; 1,000, 10,000, 100,000, Multiply by 10; 5. $50 \div (2 + 8) - 3$; 6. 30; Answers will vary. 7. $c = s - 4$; 8. multiplication; 9. $4 + 8 \div 2 - 1$; 10. 4, 8; (4, 8); 6, 12, (6, 12); 8, 16 (8, 16); 11. $y - 45$; 12. Answers will vary.

Pages 13–14

1. $(6 \times 7) - (4 + 8)$; 2. 25; 3. $a > b$; 4. 20, 24, 28, Add 4; 45, 60, 75, Add 15; $\frac{7}{8}$, $\frac{9}{8}$, $\frac{11}{8}$, Add $\frac{2}{8}$; 5. $15 - 3 + (40 \div 2) - 8$; 6. 36, Answers will vary. 7. $q = 2 \times s$; 8. addition; 9. $11 - (15 - 10) + 8$; 10. 6, 5, (6, 5); 5, 7, (5, 7); 4, 9, (4, 9); 11. $234 - e$; 12. Answers will vary.

Pages 15–18

A. 12; B. 11; C. 3; D. 13; E. 110; F. 3; G. 7; H. 13; I. 20; J. 18; K. 2; L. 3; M. 18; N. 37; O. 52; P. 10; Q. 7; R. 8; S. 9; T. 2; U. 40; V. 24; W. 6; X. 24; Y. 22; Z. 3; AA. 16; AB. 2; AC. 6; AD. 2; AE. 0; AF. 6; AG. 15; AH. 17; AI. 11; AJ. 14; AK. 20; AL. 27

Page 19

1. H; 2. E; 3. F; 4. A; 5. G; 6. B; 7. C; 8. J; 9. I; 10. D

Page 20

1. $48 \div (12 \div 4) = 16$; 2. $(20 - 6) \div 2 = 7$; 3. $4 \times (7 + 2) = 36$; 4. $(21 + 21) \div 7 = 6$; 5. $56 - (15 + 9) = 32$; 6. $35 - (17 - 11) = 29$; 7. $45 - (22 + 9) = 14$; 8. $60 \div (10 \times 3) = 2$

Page 21

1. $360 \div s$; 2. $64 \div n$; 3. $2 \times (7 - 3)$; 4. fifteen divided by the sum of two and three; 5. $(156 - b) \times 3$; 6. the difference of 45 and 15 divided by 3; 7. ten times the difference of 10 and 6; 8. $(12 - 8) \div 2$; 9. two multiplied by the sum of 17 and 2; 10. $(7 \times 6) - 22$

Page 22

1. 3, 4, (3, 4); 6, 8, (6, 8); 9, 12, (9, 12); 12, 16, (12, 16); Check students' work. 2. 3, 2, (3, 2); 6, 4, (6, 4); 9, 6, (9, 6); 12, 8, (12, 8); Check students' work. 3. 1, 3, (1, 3); 2, 6, (2, 6); 3, 9, (3, 9); 4, 12, (4, 12); Check students' work.

Pages 23–24

A. $a = b - 4$; B–C. Answers will vary. D. 4; E. $(45,300 + 892) \times 6$, Check students' work. F. $14 + (2 \times 7)$; $(7 \times 4) - 7$; G. forty divided by the sum of two and eight, 4; H. three times the difference of nine and two, 21; I. $j = 3c$ or $j = 3 \times c$; J. $3x$ or $3 \times x$; K. 25; L. 8; M. 9; N. (7, 35), (9, 45); (12, 192), (16, 768); O. multiply by 4; Answers will vary. P. add $\frac{2}{8}$; Answers will vary.

Answer Key

Pages 25–26

1. 30.33, 33.003, 33.03, 33.3, 33.333;
2. 569.4; 3. 4.6, 46, 460, 4,600; 4. 5,000 +
200 + 6 + $\left(7 \times \frac{1}{10}\right)$ + $\left(1 \times \frac{1}{100}\right)$ +
$\left(3 \times \frac{1}{1,000}\right)$; 5. 6, ones; 0.008, thousandths;
0.6, tenths; 0.08, hundredths; 200, hundreds;
6. <; 7. 42,000, 2,400, 240,000; 8. 56.2;
six hundred seventy-one and three hundredths,
600 + 70 + 1 + $\left(3 \times \frac{1}{100}\right)$; 11.008, 10 + 1
+ $\left(8 \times \frac{1}{1,000}\right)$; 407.058, four hundred seven
and fifty-eight thousandths; 9. 2,952;
10. 18,815; 11. 986; 12. 14,184; 13. 57;
14. 826; 15. 21r7; 16. 419r3; 17. 71.57;
18. 302.4; 19. 98.97; 20. 842.276;
21. $1.48; 22. 70.2; 23. 0.24; 24. 86r1

Pages 27–28

1. 7.77, 17.71, 77.077, 77.1, 77.7; 2. 3.70;
3. 700, 70, 7, 0.7; 4. 600 + 80 + 3 + $\left(4 \times \frac{1}{10}\right)$
+ $\left(2 \times \frac{1}{1,000}\right)$; 5. 7, ones; 0.05, hundredths;
0.6, tenths; 0, tens; 0.009, thousandths; 6. >;
7. 36,000, 3,600, 900,000; 8. 350.07;
thirty-four and twenty-nine thousandths,
30 + 4 + $\left(2 \times \frac{1}{100}\right)$ + $\left(9 \times \frac{1}{1,000}\right)$; 60.43,
60 + $\left(4 \times \frac{1}{10}\right)$ + $\left(3 \times \frac{1}{100}\right)$; 720.803,
seven hundred twenty and eight hundred three
thousandths; 9. 1,530; 10. 13,867; 11. 442;
12. 44,190; 13. 96r4; 14. 150r2; 15. 41;
16. 300r7; 17. 21.07; 18. 98.8; 19. 660.34;
20. 664.607; 21. $3.12; 22. 443; 23. 0.18;
24. 62r3

Pages 29–30
Matches: A, B; C, F; D, G; E, H; I, O; J, P; K, L;
M, Q; R, N

Page 31
1. 100; 2. 1,000; 3. 10,000; 4. 100,000;
5. 1,000,000; 6. 10,000,000; 7. 4, 40,
400, 4,000, 40,000; 8. 9, 90, 900, 9,000,
90,000; 9. 7.8, 78, 780, 7,800; 10. 832,
83.2, 8.32, 0.832; 11. 0.6, 6, 60, 600;
12. 1,000, 100, 10, 1; 13. 148.2, 1,482,
14,820, 148,200; 14. 620, 62, 6.2, 0.62

Answer Key

Pages 32–33
1. 434; 2. 4,338; 3. 2,432; 4. 11,535;
5. 714; 6. 2,592; 7. 5,805; 8. 157,828;
9. 38,135; 10. 240,355; 11. 917,690;
12. 728,064; 13. 3,420; 14. 285,012;
15. 1,344 textbooks; 16. 864 oz.;
17. 82,800 crayons

Pages 34–35
1. 113; 2. 147; 3. 94; 4. 80; 5. 208r1;
6. 583r4; 7. 629r2; 8. 1,363r4; 9. 46;
10. 31; 11. 202r7; 12. 59r11; 13. 30;
14. 90; 15. 90, Answers will vary.
16. 45 rows; 17. 289 dozen eggs;
18. 28 rows

Page 36
1. 29,148; 2. 21r12; 3. 16r16; 4. 4,214;
5. 106; 6. 875,524; 7. 436,449; 8. 27r18;
9. $3,060; 10. 216 pages

Page 37
1. 87.36; nine hundred and fifty-four
thousandths, $900 + \left(5 \times \frac{1}{100}\right) + \left(4 \times \frac{1}{1,000}\right)$; 4.67, $4 + \left(6 \times \frac{1}{10}\right) + \left(7 \times \frac{1}{100}\right)$; 720.702,
seven hundred twenty and seven hundred two
thousandths; 0.037, $\left(3 \times \frac{1}{100}\right) + \left(7 \times \frac{1}{1,000}\right)$; three hundred three and six tenths, $300 + 3 + \left(6 \times \frac{1}{10}\right)$; 2. 7.05, 7.49, 7.5, 7.505, 7.55;
3. 82.08, 82.8, 88, 88.008, 88.8; 4. 0.005,
0.05, 0.5, 0.505, 0.555; 5. <; 6. >; 7. <; 8.
<; 9. >; 10. >; 11. >; 12. <; 13. <; 14. =

Page 38
1. Check students' work. A. 1, B. 0, C. 0, D. 1;
2. Check students' work. A. 14, B. 16, C. 15;
D. 15; 3. Check students' work. A. 33, B. 34,
C. 33, D. 33; 4. 4,670.5; 5. 892.3; 6. 0.6;
7. 926; 8. 42; 9. 240; 10. 5.89; 11. 4.3;
12. 0.63; 13. 1; 14. 7.47, 7.5, 7; 15. 0.51,
0.5, 1

Page 42
1. 10.2; 2. 18; 3. 11.06; 4. 65.9; 5. 0.4;
6. 4; 7. 38.29; 8. 8.39; 9. 100.16; 10. 0.68;
11. 181.22; 12. 39.36; 13. 13.2 lb.;
14. 2.34 in.

Page 43
1. 50.4; 2. 17.4; 3. 38.4; 4. 74.1; 5. 133.4;
6. 312.5; 7. 421.5; 8. 620.25; 9. 6.336;
10. 3.12; 11. $5.64; 12. 4.92; 13. 11.2 in.;
14. $2.45

Page 44
1. 351.7; 2. 32.8; 3. 40; 4. 67.33; 5. 0.24;
6. 3,339.861; 7. 27.33; 8. 812.5;
9. 6.5 days; 10. 157.314 mi.

Pages 45–46
A. 0.98; B. 0.499; C. 1.2; D. 1.09; E. 0.62;
F. 0.979; G. 1.06; H. 1.027; I. 0.176;
J. 0.15; K. 0.162; L. 2; M. 0.8; N. 0.5;
O. 0.198; P. 0.8; Q. 0.128; R. 1.2; S. 1.25;
T. 1; U. 0.168

Answer Key

Pages 47–48

A. Answers will vary. B. 0.048, 0.29, 0.365, 0.39, 0.4; C. $4{,}000 + 500 + 2 + \left(3 \times \frac{1}{10}\right)$ $+ \left(4 \times \frac{1}{1{,}000}\right)$, four thousand five hundred two and three hundred four thousandths; D. Check students' work. E. \$3.33; F. \$20.82; G. \$205.14; H. 10 or 10^1, Answers will vary. I. 3, Answers will vary. J. yes, Check students' work. K. 3,744 petunias; L. about \$9; M. \$30.66; N. 55.6 mi.; O–P. Answers will vary.

Pages 49–50

1. $\frac{1}{10}$, $\frac{1}{4}$, $\frac{6}{12}$, $\frac{5}{8}$, $\frac{2}{3}$; 2. <, <, <; 3. $\frac{21}{5}$, $\frac{27}{7}$, $\frac{11}{4}$; 4. $\frac{3}{5}$, $\frac{1}{4}$, $\frac{1}{5}$; 5. Check students' work. A. 1, B. 1, C. 0, D. 1; E. 2, F. 2, G. 1, H. 2; 6. $\frac{2}{3}$; 7. $\frac{7}{8}$; 8. $\frac{1}{2}$; 9. $1\frac{1}{5}$; 10. $\frac{2}{3}$; 11. $\frac{3}{8}$; 12. $1\frac{5}{8}$; 13. 3; 14. $\frac{1}{20}$; 15. 14; 16. 3; 17. $\frac{1}{8}$; 18. 6

Pages 51–52

1. $\frac{1}{8}$, $\frac{1}{3}$, $\frac{3}{5}$, $\frac{3}{4}$, $\frac{5}{6}$; 2. >, <, <; 3. $1\frac{1}{5}$, $6\frac{1}{6}$, $6\frac{2}{3}$; 4. $\frac{1}{3}$, $\frac{1}{4}$, $\frac{2}{3}$; 5. Check students' work. A. 1, B. 0, C. 1, D. 0, E. 1, F. 2, G. 3, H. 2; 6. $\frac{2}{5}$; 7. 1; 8. $\frac{5}{8}$; 9. $1\frac{2}{3}$; 10. $1\frac{5}{12}$; 11. $\frac{3}{10}$; 12. $1\frac{1}{6}$; 13. $\frac{1}{2}$; 14. $\frac{1}{15}$; 15. 7; 16. 16; 17. $\frac{1}{4}$; 18. 12

Pages 53–54

A. $\frac{5}{8}$; B. $\frac{3}{4}$; C. $\frac{1}{2}$; D. $1\frac{1}{12}$; E. $1\frac{5}{12}$; F. $\frac{13}{24}$; G. $\frac{7}{8}$; H. $\frac{3}{8}$; I. $\frac{1}{3}$; J. $\frac{1}{5}$; K. $\frac{7}{12}$; L. $\frac{3}{8}$; M. $\frac{1}{2}$; N. $\frac{19}{30}$; O. $3\frac{5}{8}$; P. $1\frac{5}{6}$; Q. $4\frac{3}{8}$; R. $2\frac{5}{12}$; S. $2\frac{7}{10}$; T. $1\frac{1}{8}$; U. $3\frac{9}{10}$

Page 55

1. $\frac{9}{10}$; 2. $\frac{6}{10}$ or $\frac{3}{5}$; 3. $\frac{82}{100}$ or $\frac{41}{50}$; 4. $\frac{3}{6}$ or $\frac{1}{2}$; 5. $1\frac{1}{8}$; 6. $\frac{2}{4}$ or $\frac{1}{2}$; 7. $\frac{15}{100}$ or $\frac{3}{20}$; 8. $\frac{5}{8}$; 9. $\frac{1}{6}$; 10. $\frac{9}{10}$; 11. $\frac{1}{12}$; 12. 7; 13. 1; 14. 2; 15. 2

Page 56

1. 2, $\frac{10}{3}$; 2. $\frac{2}{15}$; 3. $\frac{1}{2}$; 4. $1\frac{1}{3}$; 5. $1\frac{1}{3}$; 6. $3\frac{3}{10}$; 7. $\frac{2}{9}$ sq. m; 8. $\frac{2}{5}$ sq. ft.; 9. $\frac{3}{10}$ sq. yd.; 10. $5\frac{1}{3}$ mi.; 11. $2\frac{2}{3}$ packs; 12. $\frac{3}{10}$ of the cake, Check students' work.

Pages 57–58

A. $\frac{3}{7}$; B. $\frac{1}{12}$; C. $\frac{1}{8}$; D. $3\frac{3}{4}$; E. $1\frac{1}{3}$; F. $\frac{2}{15}$; G. $\frac{3}{14}$; H. 8; I. $2\frac{1}{2}$; J. $\frac{5}{9}$; K. $\frac{5}{16}$; L. $2\frac{2}{5}$; M. $1\frac{7}{8}$; N. $\frac{1}{8}$; O. $\frac{1}{5}$; P. $2\frac{5}{8}$; Q. $\frac{4}{5}$; R. $4\frac{1}{2}$; S. $\frac{5}{12}$; T. $\frac{1}{5}$; U. $\frac{4}{15}$

Page 59

1. <; 2. >; 3. <; 4. <; 5. =; 6. >; 7. $2 \times \frac{3}{4}$; 8. $\frac{1}{4} \times \frac{2}{3}$; 9. $\frac{5}{5} \times \frac{7}{5}$; 10. It will be less since the other factor is less than 1.

Answer Key

Page 60

1. 3; 2. 9; 3–4. Check students' work.

5. $\frac{1}{3}$ cookie; 6. $\frac{3}{4}$ candy bar; 7. $1\frac{1}{5}$ minutes or

1 minute 12 seconds; 8. $\frac{2}{3}$ of an hour or

40 minutes

Page 61

1–2. Check students' work. 3. $1\frac{1}{4}$ candy bar,

$5 \div 4$, $\frac{5}{4}$; 4. $\frac{1}{6}$ sandwich; 5. 15 burgers;

6. 32 truffles

Page 62

1. $\frac{1}{4}$ of the field; 2. $\frac{5}{12}$ of the room;

3. 24 muffins; 4. $\frac{3}{8}$ of the bag; 5. $\frac{11}{20}$ of the

blanket

Pages 63–64

A. Check students' work. B. Answers will vary

but may include $\frac{2}{6}$, $\frac{4}{12}$, or $\frac{8}{24}$. C. $\frac{1}{5}$, $\frac{25}{100}$, $\frac{1}{2}$,

$\frac{3}{4}$, $\frac{4}{5}$; D. 4, 1, $\frac{1}{4}$, $\frac{1}{8}$; E. Answers will vary.

F. $7\frac{11}{12}$ mi.; G. $\frac{7}{20}$ of the project; H. 14 bows;

I. 4 laps; J. $\frac{3}{4}$ of a brownie; K. $\frac{3}{10}$ of the goal;

L. $13\frac{1}{3}$ sq. yd.; M. Check students' work.

N. Check students' work. $\frac{1}{15}$; O. Check

students' work. $\frac{4}{10}$ or $\frac{2}{5}$; P. 7:05

Pages 65–66

1. =; 2. >; 3. >; 4. 1; 5. 12; 6. 3; 7. 5 mm,

5 cm, 5 m; 8. 130 in., 12 ft., 5 yd.;

9. 9,000 sec., 170 min., 3 hr.; 10. 5 qt.,

13 pt., 30 cups, 2 gal.; 11. 12 times;

12. $21\frac{1}{4}$ mi.; 13. 2 mi.; 14. 6 days; 15. 3, 3,

3, 27; 16. 9 cubic units; 17. 72 ft.^{3}; 18. 190

cm^3; 19. 9 gal.; 20. 64 ft.^{3}

Pages 67–68

1. <; 2. <; 3. >; 4. 7,000; 5. 10; 6. 3;

7. 4 in., 4 ft., 4 yd., 4 mi.; 8. 6 pt., 15 cups,

1 gal., 5 qt.; 9. 1,000 mm, 1 km, 1,200 m;

10. 3,500 sec., 1 hr., 80 min.; 11. $6\frac{1}{4}$ in.;

12. 4 days; 13. $\frac{1}{2}$ in.; 14. 3 days; 15. 2, 3, 5,

30; 16. 12 units^3; 17. 112 in.^{3}; 18. 248 in.^{3};

19. 1,926 in.; 20. 512 in.^{3}

Pages 69–70

Matches: A, D; B, H; C, E; F, I; G, P; J, N; K, L;
M, O; Q, AJ; R, AC; S, X; T, AG; U, Y; Z, AA;
V, AB; W, AI; AD, AE; AF, AH

Page 71

1. liter; 2. 2; 3. kilometer; 4. 60; 5. 1, 3, 16,
10, 26; 6. 3, 6, 14,000, 24,000, 40,000;
7. 1,000, 4, 7,000, 9, 15; 8. 3,600 g, 3 kg;
9. 5,500 lb., 3 T.; 10. C

Page 72

1. 10; 2. 3; 3. 5; 4. 7; 5. $\frac{5}{8}$ lb.; 6. $\frac{4}{8}$ or $\frac{1}{2}$ lb.;

7. $4\frac{1}{8}$ lb.

Answer Key

Page 73

1. Check students' work. 2. $5\frac{3}{4}$ lb., $6\frac{3}{4}$ lb.;
3. 1 lb.; 4. 10; 5. $60\frac{3}{4}$ lb.; 6. $5\frac{3}{4}$ lb.;
7. 4, Answers will vary.

Page 74

1. bottom; 2. top; 3. top; 4. 15; 5. 6, 4, 5, 120; 6. Answers will vary.

Page 75

1. 16; 2. 20; 3. 4, 3, 3, 36; 4. 5, 5, 5, 125; 5. 3, 3, 3, 27 units^3; 6. 3, 3, 5, 45 units^3; 7. Answers will vary.

Page 76

1. 80 ft.^{3}; 2. 160 mi.^{3}; 3. 60 m^3; 4. 1,000 cm^3; 5. 3 mi.; 6. 4 m

Page 77

1. 180 ft.^{3}; 2. 224 mi.^{3}; 3. 72 mm^3; 4. 14 cm^3; 5. 228 in.^{3}; 6. 690 cm^3

Page 78

1. 5 in.; 2. 12 ft.^{3}; 3. 960 ft.^{3}; 4. Students should shade to the 2 inch mark. Answers will vary. 5. 5,184 ft.^{3}, Check students' work.

Pages 79–80

A. 8 cm^3; B. 2 ft.; C. 880, 3,220, 3,450; D. 7, 1,800, 1,500; E. 60, 22, 6; F. 55,000 g, 6.6 kg, 100,000 g; G. 640, 650, 5.5; H. 9, 7, 4; I. 4 days; J. tank A; Answers will vary. K. 4 gal.; L. Answers will vary. Check students' work. M. the first bed; N. 96 in.^{3}; O–P. Check students' work.

Page 81

1 Check students' work. 2. (2, 5), (4, 5), (2, 3), (4, 3); 3. Check students' work. Answers will vary. 4. trapezoids; 5. rectangle, square, Check students' work.

Page 82

1. Check students' work. 2. (1, 1), (1, 5), (5, 1), (5, 5); 3. Check students' work. Answers will vary. 4. pentagons; 5. Answers will vary but may include squares, rectangles, parallelograms, and rhombuses. Check students' workk.

Pages 83–84

1. E; 2. B; 3. trapezoid; 4. (1, 5); 5. Check students' work. 6. (2, 1), (5, 8), (0, 0), (6, 9), (0, 10); 7. (2, 2); 8. right triangle; 9. 12 in., Check students' work. 10. John's; 11. (6, 4), Check students' work. 12. 4, (2, 4), 6, (3, 6), 8, (4, 8), 10, (5, 10), 12, (6, 12), 14, (7, 14), 16, (8, 16), Check students' work.

Pages 85–86

1. 8, 8, 5, 5, 4, 4, 6, 6, Check students' work. 2. rhombus; 3. False; 4. False; 5. False; 6. False; 7. True; 8. Check students' work. 9. True; 10. False; 11. True; 12. True; 13. scalene, isosceles, equilateral; 14. Check students' work.

Pages 89–90

A–B. Check students' work. C. (4, 9); D. (5, 7); E. (5, 3); F. Check students' work. G. right or scalene; H–J. Check students' work. K. square, rectangle; Check students' work. L. True, Check students' work. M. Check students' work. N. square; O. four sides and four right angles; A square has four equal sides. P. four equal sides; A square has to have four right angles.